European Spoons
Before 1700

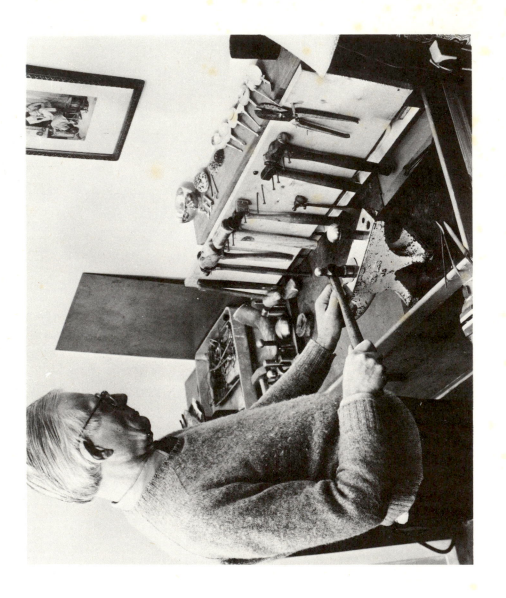

The author at work on a diamond-point spoon. The twenty-eight pound anvil is about the minimum weight for the job, the selection of hammers and mallets seen more than adequate. The reflections from the bowl and the spoons on the shelf show the finish obtained from the hammer, followed by a light rub over with metal polish.

European Spoons
Before 1700

JOHN EMERY

M.A.(Cantab.)

JOHN DONALD PUBLISHERS LTD

EDINBURGH

ISBN 0 85976 012 X

Printed and bound in Great Britain by
Morrison & Gibb Ltd., London and Edinburgh

Illustrations

IN selecting illustrations, the intention has been to make them as fully representative as possible. This has resulted in three different categories. The first contains professional pictures of spoons which were readily accessible—some taken by leading museums and auction rooms, and others specially for this book. The second contains spoons which were photographed by the author in the course of several extensive European tours; this involved working, often in a hurry, in conditions ranging from the mid-day sun in Venice to the basement of a museum in the Hague, with a small camera built for the purpose, but without proper lighting equipment: the results are variable, and some backgrounds have had to be blocked out. The third category comprises line drawings, in almost every case made by the author from photographs which were too poor to print; these were traced full size, and are as accurate as the thickness of a pencil point will allow, but in some cases the originals were so worn or corroded that detail, particularly of engraved ornament, cannot be guaranteed. In making these diagrams, obvious accidental damage has been restored.

In a few instances, replicas of spoons have been illustrated instead of the originals; these replicas have been made by the author from careful measurements and photographs, and were thought to give a better idea of what the originals looked like when in use than the worn and corroded fragments which now remain.

Except where otherwise stated, all illustrations are reproduced three-quarters full size: lengths in centimetres and weights in grams have been given where known.

References

REFERENCES to literature are numbered for each section separately, the list being printed at the end of the section. Works referred to, together with others which are relevant to the study of spoons, are cited in the general bibliography. The list does not claim to be complete, but contains everything which has come to the author's notice.

Location of Specimens

LOCATIONS are given only for those specimens which are in museums open to the public; others may be in private collections, or were photographed for sale catalogues, or in shops.

In many cases, the spoons illustrated are not normally on view, but museum authorities are in general very helpful about producing them on request.

Acknowledgements

I have learned much from the works listed in the bibliography, but perhaps more in the course of conversation and correspondence with people all over Europe, many of whom have given much valuable time to answering questions and displaying specimens.

I am especially indebted to Th. M. Duyvene de Wit Klinkhamer, formerly of the Rijksmuseum, who first put me in touch with sources of information, and to Mr Karel Citroen of Amsterdam, whose comments, particularly on the subject of fakes, have been of the greatest value. It has been a most pleasant experience to be allowed complete freedom everywhere to examine and photograph specimens, and I shall not forget the owner of a small shop in Leeuwarden who offered an early spoon for sale. I said that I would like to consult the Director of the Fries Museum about it, and suggested leaving my passport with him meanwhile. He replied: 'No, it is all right; you are English, you will come back.' I most sincerely hope that no compatriot of mine will ever give him cause to revise his opinion.

Particular thanks are due also to the following:

Mr J. S. Forbes, Deputy Warden, The Worshipful Company of Goldsmiths.
Mr C. C. Oman, formerly of the Victoria and Albert Museum.
The late Dr N. M. Penzer.
Mrs How (of How of Edinburgh).
Mr Michael Clayton (of Christie, Manson and Woods).
Mr Richard Came (of Sotheby and Co.).
Mr P. Lazko, formerly of the British Museum.
Mr Michael Wellby.
Mr N. Gorevic.
The late Mr M. Blank.
The late Mr Harry Freeman.
Dr Richard Nicholls, of the Fitzwilliam Museum, Cambridge.
Mr Nicholas Thomas, of the City Museum, Birmingham.
Mr George Hart, silversmith, of Chipping Campden.
Mr Ian Finlay, formerly Director of the Royal Scottish Museum, and Mr Malcolm Baker.
Messrs R. Stevenson, Stuart Maxwell, David Caldwell and Hugh McKerall of the National Museum of Antiquities of Scotland.
Dr J. E. Whitley, of the Scottish Research Reactor Centre.
Mr T. R. Mulder, of the Westfries Museum, Hoorn.
Mr W. Helveg, spoonmaker, of Amsterdam.

Mr W. Heerens, silversmith, of Schoonhoven.
Mr Jan Elders, silversmith, of Hoorn.
Dr Beatrice Jansen and Dr Jean Gallois, of the Gemeente Museum, the Hague.
The Director and staff of the Fries Museum, Leeuwarden, and of Groningen Museum.
Mr P. Voet, of Haarlem.
The late Mr J. W. Frederiks, of the Hague.
The Conservateur, the Curtius Museum, Liege.
Hr. Bodo Glaub, of Cologne.
Sr. G. Bianci, silversmith, of Florence.
Prof. Santangelo, of Rome.
Donna Zenaide Giunta, of Messrs Bulgari, Rome.
Prof. J. B. Ward Perkins, formerly Director of the British School, Rome.
Sna. Nardella Elsa, Torre Annunciata.
Sr. Matteo Bono, of Camping Quai, Iseo.
The Director of the Museum of Brescia.
Dott. Maria Zecchinelli, of the Museo Civico, Como.
M. Marc Segal, of Berne.
Dr Sigurd Schoubye, of Tonder.
Mrs Fritz Lindahl, of the Nationalmuseet, Copenhagen.
Dr Inger-Marie Kwaal Lie, of the Kunstindustriemuseet, Oslo.
Dr Bechstein, of the Germanisches Museum, Nuremberg.
Dr Friederike Prodinger, of the Salzburg Museum.
Dr Jĭrí Neustupny, of the National Museum, Prague.
Padre Carmelo Onãte Guillén, S.J., of Valladolid.

Contents

1

Introduction

SPOONS are tools used for eating what cannot conveniently be held in the fingers or drunk from a cup; to select them as a subject of study may seem unambitious. However, second only to knives, they are among the oldest, as well as the most personal, of man's implements. A spoon is often the first present to a new baby, by a custom which was well over a thousand years old when Shakespeare made Henry VIII upbraid Cranmer for his unwillingness to sponsor the infant Elizabeth—

'Come come, my lord, you'd spare your spoons—';

it is traditionally the first item in a prospective bride's bottom drawer; it figures in the christening of infants, the crowning of kings and the Communion rite of Churches; it is the symbol of courtship, the emblem of rank of a Jutish lady, and the subject of nursery rhymes, proverbs and fables too numerous to recall; the devil may carry a fork, but whoso sups with him must have a full long spoon.

The history of a simple object is rarely simple. In the average family spoon drawer can be found the result of a blending of Roman and Norman, Crusader and Saracen. The marks which today distinguish silver from plate have their origin in a Christian emblem, the dishonesty of company officials and the reckless finances of a much-married king, and to the making of spoons have been brought most of the useful arts of mankind.

Many books, and not a few monographs, have been written about the spoons of England, but none about those of Europe as a whole; the account which follows is an attempt to make good this deficiency. It does not claim to be complete, and that for two good reasons: the first is that for England and Scotland, Norway, Sweden and Denmark there exist good accounts, and the spoons of these countries have been dealt with here only because these accounts—and indeed spoons—are rather inaccessible. The second is that it would take an interminable time to deal with every country, and it seemed better to have an account of some than no account at all. Much of what is contained here is fundamental to all spoons and all countries and provides a foundation on which further study can be based.

The writer has been interested in spoons for some thirty years. This interest has taken the form of collecting on a limited scale, studying every available specimen, book and picture, and last—but not least—making every kind of spoon in order to find out how it could have been made (not quite the same thing as how it was made, but the best that one can do), what it was useful for, how well it lasted—and how the genuine could be distinguished from the fake.

1

When, after repeated attempts to re-discover the methods of long-dead craftsmen, one can produce something which will make the experts think twice, one appreciates the difficulty of being absolutely certain about some pieces, but this is offset by a high degree of confidence about others. From time to time, the assistance of university acquaintances armed with the most sophisticated modern analytical equipment has been sought, and a margin of uncertainty remains.

Some particular problems which have been encountered might be mentioned here, not by way of excuse, but as a qualification to some statements made and a caution against accepting them unquestioningly.

Apart from those which date themselves by their hallmarks, contemporary inscriptions or recorded history, the vast majority of spoons examined can only be dated by a combination of circumstantial evidence and intelligent conjecture. Very few have been dug up in properly organised archaeological investigations and, invaluable as these few are, even then the date of burial fixes only a minimum age. By their nature, buried deposits of precious metal objects represent generally either the family treasures accumulated over a considerable period of time or the proceeds of indiscriminate pillage over a wide area—the Mildenhall treasure (in the British Museum) being an example of the first and the Traprain Law treasure (in the National Museum of Antiquities of Scotland) an example of the second. Sometimes the fortuitous association of objects can lead to erroneous conclusions, as in the case of the spoon and fork in the St Ninian's treasure (National Museum of Antiquities of Scotland), which are so different in conception and execution as to leave little doubt that they came from different cultural provinces, but whose association led to the propounding of the untenable theory that the treasure as a whole is a coherent ecclesiastical assemblage.

One could cite numerous examples of situations making for bewilderment. Two bronze spoons dug up by the owner on a site near Lake Iseo (north of Brescia) were attributed by the Milan museum authorities to the Augustan age: exact duplicates in the Victoria and Albert museum are labelled as seventeenth century. A pair of brass spoons in the Musée des Arts Décoratifs in Paris are exhibited on two separate floors, one as German and the other as Dutch, attributed to different centuries. And in Italy, the designation 'Roman—dug up in the forum' is found attached to spoons made during more than a millennium.

The attitude of individuals also varies widely. In Britain and in Holland the unfailing courtesy and co-operation of museum staff enhances one's confidence in human nature, but their example is not followed everywhere.

Finally there is the problem of looking up references. Living in the country, fifty miles from a major library and over four hundred from a really comprehensive one, it is difficult to do justice to all written sources. The difficulty is not diminished by the fact that these are in at least ten European languages. It would be surprising in these circumstances if something relevant had not been missed. Equally, it is difficult always to be sure where or from whom one first came by a piece of information, and if references have occasionally been omitted, I apologise to those concerned.

This survey of European spoons was made possible by the generosity of the Goldsmiths' Company of London, to whom I am deeply indebted; for the rest, I owe a great deal to the staff of museums in this country and abroad, who have been most helpful and encouraging; to the members of the trade, who are sources not only of spoons but of information; to the staff of the leading auction rooms, who have been very patient with me; and finally, to my wife, family and friends, who have put up with a spoon-laden atmosphere, eaten with the oddest miscellany of implements, and lived with the sound of hammer on anvil as one of the ordinary household noises. All these I have known as persons, but there are others whom I have not known—the writers of books, into whose labours I have entered. Last of all I would like to thank the makers of the spoons themselves, without whose ingenuity and craftsmanship our tables would have been so much less elegant and interesting and this book would never have been conceived.

2

Of Spoons in General

CLASSIFICATION

IT is very difficult to draw up a completely logical scheme for classifying objects as diverse as spoons, and it is unlikely that any one attempt will suit everybody. Previous works have concentrated on material, shape and purpose. Any one of the three, taken by itself, leads to the separation of nearly identical articles and the grouping together of radically different ones. Classification by country of origin, implicit in a number of works, is even worse, since not only are the products of different countries frequently almost indistinguishable, but the political changes of historical times make the designations of today quite unsuitable for dealing with products of a few centuries ago.

In the account which follows, shape and material are given due consideration, but considerable emphasis is placed on the way in which a given shape is achieved. Craftsmen are notoriously conservative in the matter of processes, whilst not unwilling to conform with fashion in the matter of products. This basis of classification succeeds very largely in bringing together the work of a particular period and region.

Occasionally a group of spoons show so clearly their common ancestry that they deserve a category to themselves: this is the case only rarely, the outstanding example being the Dutch hoof-ends and related types of the seventeenth century.

Sellers and buyers of spoons frequently describe them primarily in terms of their finials. This may be useful when market price is the main consideration, but leads to many absurdities. The bowls and stems of English apostle, seal-top and lion-sejant spoons differ only in the most minor details, if at all, and all three types were made at the same time, by the same makers. English and Dutch apostle spoons, on the other hand, are fundamentally different, and the processes used to make the one would have been regarded as outlandish by the maker of the other.

The use to which a spoon was put necessarily influenced its shape. Unfortunately, there is often considerable difference of opinion as to what certain early spoons were for, and this makes classification based on use a very uncertain business, but this does not mean that the purpose is unimportant. Early spoons are nowadays generally objects on a shelf, frequently behind glass, and are liable to be worn, corroded and almost too precious to handle. To have any understanding of them one must realise that each was made by one man, so that another could eat a particular kind of food from a particular vessel according to the manners of the times. It is all too easy to become very learned about morphology and quite blind to the factors underlying it. The gradual changes which have influenced spoons have reflected changes in diet, in manners, in the availability of materials and the techniques used to handle them, in political outlook and social organisation—in fact, in the whole history of man.

Whatever the shortcomings of what follows, one claim—perhaps unusual in a work of this kind—can be made. Whenever it is said that a spoon could or could not have been made in a certain way, or used for a certain purpose, what is being stated is not just an opinion, but the result of an experiment. The writer has made and used spoons of almost every known type, with a wide variety of materials and tools and for most major kinds of food. When it is asserted that the Iona spoons could have been for general domestic use, it is because a very exact copy has so been used, and comments about the way in which a particular effect might have been achieved are the aftermath of considerable thought and labour in achieving it. It is not always possible to determine exactly how something *was* done, but it is at least helpful to know how it might have been done.

Shape

The bowl of a spoon can have several functions, but there are two limiting ones. The first is that of a small cup, from the edge of which a liquid can be drunk; the second is that of a shovel, on which relatively dry food can be carried to the mouth. Many spoons are used for both, but the compromise is seldom really satisfactory. In polite society one is expected to drink soup from the side of the bowl of a large spoon, and to eat porridge from the tip of a small one, but the presence of solid lumps in the soup, or complete liquefaction of the porridge, bring out the specialised character of the two spoons used. For liquids a shallow, level-edged bowl with a radius of curvature of about 3–4·5 centimetres is desirable (the same radius as in an average cup): for solids the tip should have a radius of between 1 and 2·5 centimetres, anything bigger being awkward to put into the mouth. Modern spoons tend to combine the two functions by having pointed oval bowls, but a return to specialisation is apparent in the round-bowled soup spoons (bouillon spoons in the U.S.A.) and very pointed grape-fruit spoons which are found in many modern services.

There are early spoons approximating to the limits of both types. The round-bowled spoons made in Hoorn in the mid-seventeenth century are only usable for liquids, while the leaf-shaped bowls of the Iona spoons are excellent for porridge but quite useless for soup—as are the strongly curved bowls of the typical English apostle spoons of the sixteenth century (Fig. 1).

Next to bowl shape comes the angle between bowl and stem, and here the shape of the container is all important: the stem can be held almost horizontally if it is used from a plate, but must be tilted to eat from a bowl. The changes which occur in English spoons between 1450 and 1650 strongly suggest a growing use of pewter plates instead of wooden bowls.

The shape of the stem is the most variable quantity in spoon design: it must fit the hand, but the human hand is very adaptable, and manages to grasp a wide variety of shapes. At least two different grips can be used, the normal English manner with the stem roughly parallel with the thumb and first two fingers, and one in which the tip of the stem is held under the thumb and at right angles to it. Experiments suggest that the latter was used for all mediaeval spoons, and certainly for the Italian and Dutch hoof ends, which are almost uncontrollable in any other way. The suggestion that adults ate from spoons with the stem clenched in the fist should be made the basis of experiments before it is accepted.

One more factor seems relevant to classification. Some spoons are clearly meant for everyday use by ordinary people; others are for special occasions, but still in ordinary families; a third group contains spoons which are too complicated, too expensive or too fragile to be either useful or representative, and into this group go many cherished museum specimens—spoons with bowls of thin shell, or of rock-crystal, with stems of coral or filigree work and similar extravagances. These may be impressive feats of craftsmanship, but they have little relevance to the development of spoons as a whole.

MANUFACTURE

Under this heading spoons may be divided into four major classes—those which utilise naturally occurring objects, those which are carved from the solid, those made of metal, and those formed from material in a plastic condition, such as glass or clay, subsequently hardened.

Natural objects

The favourite raw material in this class is shell—either of the genus Cyprea (cowrie) or one of the pearly shells: a few are suitable as found, but most require to be sawn across and rubbed down on a stone, after which they can be mounted on stems of wood, bone or metal. Such spoons are found from at least 1400 B.C. to the present day (Figs. 2 and 5).

Another much-used material is horn; strongly curved horns, such as those of sheep and goats, if suitably cut, provide excellent spoon bowls of oval shape, with enough of a tang to bind into a stem made of wood, or of another horn, or of bone, reed or metal. Larger horns can be softened by boiling and then pressed into shape, stem and bowl in one piece.[1] Both types are found, the former nowadays in Turkey and formerly among the Indians of America, and the latter in Scotland, where the long-horned Highland cattle provide excellent raw material. Tortoiseshell treated in much the same manner has been used in Turkey in comparatively recent times (Figs. 3 and 81).

A study of the metal spoons of Europe leads one to believe that many varieties derive from prototypes having horn bowls, but these have not often been preserved; horn spoons of any great age are naturally rare.

A few spoons are known, chiefly from Scotland, made from suitably shaped bones of sea-birds; they are primitive, and not of much historical importance.

Carvings

Wood, bone, ivory and stone spoons are all made by carving from the solid. The first three can be treated together, as the methods are very similar, and involve only simple tools.[2] To be reasonably thin, yet strong, a curly-grained wood such as burr maple is desirable, but boxwood and even beech have been used—the latter is of course still employed for cooking spoons. Spoons with bowls and stems of burr maple, tipped with silver, are not uncommon from Germany and Switzerland; they are short, and some may well have been made out of the waste from turning mazer bowls (Figs. 3, 92 and 94).

The carving of bone and ivory follows the same lines as for wood, but the material can be cut thinner; few bones are thick enough to provide a really good bowl depth, such as is needed in a soup spoon, but bone egg spoons have a very respectably long history. The rarity of ivory makes spoons of this material uncommon, and they cannot have had much effect on the history of spoons in general.

Stone, chiefly rock-crystal, but also jade, agate and lapis lazuli, was used for spoon bowls in the late Renaissance period, chiefly in Italy. These hard stones can only be cut by a slow grinding process, the expense of which made it worth while to mount the bowls on elaborate gold or silver-gilt stems. Such spoons must always have been uncommon and, being individual works of art, they do not necessarily reflect current styles in other materials; they were probably mostly made as expensive presents.

Metal

To carve a spoon from a solid block of metal would be possible but ridiculous; two processes may be used to shape either the separate parts or the whole—casting and forging.

In casting, liquid metal is poured into a solid mould and allowed to set; this is normally the first stage in making anything of metal, but when one speaks of a casting one means something cast into very nearly its final form, as opposed to something subsequently shaped by cutting or hammering.

Casting can be done into permanent moulds, made of stone, baked clay or metal, and these have been used from the earliest times; the need to get the finished object out imposes certain obvious limitations of shape, and it is difficult to find stone capable of taking fine detail and yet withstanding the temperatures required to melt gold or silver, but for simple shapes, and especially for metals with relatively low melting points, stone moulds are very successful. They were used by the Greeks for casting fibula brooches, which are very like spoons in shape, and it seems likely that they were used in classical times for spoons also. They were certainly employed in Scandinavia in Viking and mediaeval times.[3]

Baked clay moulds produce similar results to those of stone; metal has not often been used for anything but rough ingots in silver, but was certainly employed for casting pewter, as it still is.

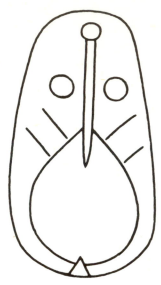

Half of a clay mould for a spoon of mediaeval type. After Oldeberg—see Bibliography.
Approximately half full size.

A disadvantage of permanent moulds is the large amount of work locked up in them, which restricts the number of patterns of article likely to be produced; this restriction is avoided with temporary moulds, which are made in two ways.

The earliest method was to model the article in wax, which was then embedded in a suitable clay or other plastic material; when this had set hard and dry the mould was heated, allowing the wax to run out, and the molten metal was poured in to take its place. This, the *cire perdue* process, was perfected in the third millennium B.C. and has been used ever since for producing the finest cast work; a new wax pattern is needed for each article, but this can be made by pressing the warmed wax into a plaster or metal master-mould—a device certainly used in Egypt in Imperial Roman times, and currently employed by the makers of gas turbine engines for producing turbine blading in heat-resisting metals. The process is slow and expensive, but enables spoon bowls to be cast very thin, and gives extremely fine detail. The spoons of Pompeii were probably made in this way.

A variant of this process in which slabs of clay were employed in conjunction with permanent metal patterns is described in detail by Biringuccio as in use in Milan about 1430.[4] It was slower than sand moulding, but because the clay was subsequently baked, and the metal poured while it was hot, it enabled thin sections to be cast. Early mediaeval Italian spoons were almost certainly produced thus, although Biringuccio does not specifically mention them.

Some time probably in the fourteenth or fifteenth century the process of sand casting was invented.[5] The sand, very fine, loamy, and slightly damp, is contained in two open-faced boxes, or flasks, fitted together with dowels, and the pattern is embedded between them; they are separated to remove it—and it must be of such a shape that it can be removed; after putting them together again molten metal is poured in through suitable channels. It is not practicable to heat the mould, and the metal becomes chilled on contact with it, which makes it impossible to cast such thin sections as can be obtained with the dry and hot lost-wax moulds. The finish depends on the sand, but can be made very smooth if the mould is smoked with a pitch or turpentine flame before assembly (Fig. 6).

The sand process is now almost universal for general metal casting: it was probably first used for spoons in Italy, and many late Renaissance examples of bronze appear to have been cast in one piece in this way. Silver is more difficult to handle, and one-piece silver spoons always have unduly thick bowls; the cast metal is soft and brittle, and it is for this reason that Italian silver spoons were made with cast stems, soldered to bowls hammered from plate, while bronze ones of identical form were cast in one piece.

Silver and gold can be joined with solders which differ little in composition or melting point from the parent metal. Such joints are strong and sometimes very difficult to detect, and make it possible to build up a spoon from two or more pieces. The process has the disadvantage that it involves heating the metal to redness, and this leaves it soft. It is rather often employed to join a thin bowl to a much thicker stem, and the sudden change in cross-section leads to a very high stress concentration at the junction, frequently resulting in fatigue fracture after some years of use; this can be avoided by good design, but the softening remains, and largely accounts for the fact that the soldered construction has been superseded by the process of forging in one piece.

Forging

In forging, a thick blank, usually a short length of bar or a strip cut from thick sheet, is shaped by repeated hammering; this spreads the metal, enabling thickness to be controlled, and also rearranges the internal structure, resulting in a great increase in strength.

Forged spoons have been made in two basic ways. In the first, all blows are delivered at right angles to the plane of a sheet, which must therefore be thick enough to form the thickest parts; ornament in low relief can be produced by hammering into a die. This, which will be referred to as flat forging, is the simplest method, and lends itself to mechanisation, in which part of the hammering is replaced by rolling. In the second process, blows may be delivered at any angle to the surface of the original blank, giving far greater control over shape and thickness, particularly in the stem; it is a highly skilled procedure, slow, expensive, and unsurpassable for producing good spoons, and will be referred to as forging in the round.

Flat forging was used for mediaeval brass and silver spoons of northern Europe and some of those made in Italy, the mid-seventeenth century trefids, and most spoons made from 1800 onwards; forging in the round was introduced into Italy apparently about 1300, and thence spread to the rest of Europe, being employed in England to the exclusion of other methods between 1400 and 1660, and again throughout the eighteenth century. Modern spoons are mechanically flat-forged by methods which endeavour, with only partial success, to reproduce the results of forging in the round (Fig. 7).

Soldering can be used to build up spoons from components bent or hammered from relatively thin sheet, and this was done during the seventeenth century in Friesland, Germany and Switzerland; the resulting spoons have hollow stems, and appear to be copies of earlier ones made of wood or horn. It is a difficult method of construction, with very doubtful advantages, and did not remain in vogue for long (Fig. 8). A rather different built-up construction appears to have been used in some early seventeenth-century Scandinavian spoons, the bowl and stem being separate pieces joined by a long scarfed soldered joint before being finally hammered to shape and thickness; this avoids the disadvantage of softening, since the hammering restores the hardness of the metal, and is really an easy way of making a blank.

A soldered joint is not really desirable between bowl and stem, where the loading is greatest, but is more innocuous when used to join a finial to the end of a stem; usually the joint is either halved or made as a V, but sometimes—especially in Holland—a plain butt joint was used. The finial itself is usually cast, although in some Scandinavian spoons it is fabricated from sheet.

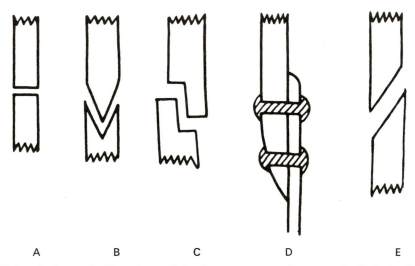

A   B   C   D   E

Types of joint. A : butt ; B : V or dovetail (an incorrect use of the term) ; C : halved ; D : riveted ; E : scarfed.

Riveted joints are occasionally used in spoons, and are almost essential when joining metal to other materials such as shell or stone; screwed joints are rare, and when found are to enable the spoon to be stowed in a small case, rather than a primary structural feature.

Both glass and ceramic materials have been used for spoons from very early times: the former can be manipulated while soft into virtually any shape, or pressed into a mould. The latter is generally formed by pressing the moist clay into a plaster mould, from which it separates easily on drying, but freehand modelling is also possible. The disadvantage in both cases is the brittleness of the finished article, necessitating rather thick sections if it is to survive in use. Spoons of this group are rare.

This brief survey of constructional methods will, it is hoped, make the accounts which follow comprehensible. It is not meant as a manual of instruction for spoon makers, and for more technical details suitable works may be consulted. Unfortunately there does not appear to be an account of forging in the round anywhere, and so one is given in an appendix, but most of the other processes are very well dealt with in the literature cited.

HALLMARKING

The ease with which base metals can be either coated with gold or silver, or used to dilute them, has been exploited by those wishing to make an easy profit from at least the time of Archimedes—one of whose famous contributions to physics was made as the result of being set the task of detecting such a fraud by his king's goldsmith. As early as the sixth century control stamps were being used in Byzantium, presumably only applied after the metal had been officially tested for quality: many of these are reproduced in Rosenberg, Vol. IV.

In Western Europe an official system of marking was instituted first in France in the late thirteenth century; shortly afterwards a statute of Edward I (Act 28, 1300) laid down a standard of 92·5% silver, and entrusted the Wardens of Goldsmiths' Hall with its enforcement; it also laid down the mark to be used, of a leopard's head. Nearly eighty years later it was made obligatory for the maker to put his own mark on the work before submitting it for test.

The Wardens were clearly not always above suspicion, for in 1478 a further mark, of a letter, was added to enable the year in which a piece had been assayed to be ascertained. This has had the quite unintended effect of making fully marked English silver exactly dateable; finally, in 1544, the mark of a lion was added to indicate that silver plate, unlike Henry VIII's coinage, was still of the 92·5% or sterling standard.

The practice of enforcing standards by official testing and marking was subsequently adopted by other countries, and the marks themselves, by their association with Goldsmiths' Hall, are known as hallmarks. The methods of testing, the standards enforced and the marks themselves varied greatly from country to country, and often within provinces of the same country, with the result that there exists an immense number of marks, the decipherment of which continues to give trouble to experts. Many attempts have been made to gather all known marks for one country into a reference work, outstanding examples being Sir Charles Jackson's *English Goldsmiths and their marks* for Britain, and the works of Elias Voet on the marks of Holland. In view of the size and complexity of these books, the idea of producing a reference work for the whole of Europe might appear fantastic, but two attempts—by Rosenberg and by Tardy—have met with considerable success.

The existence of official marks led to a whole crop of unofficial ones, employed by makers in small towns who did not wish to incur the delay and risk involved in sending their work to legally constituted assay offices; these generally look something like official marks. and are put in the right places, but there is hardly any record to show who used them or where. They occur more frequently on spoons than on anything else.

Occasionally the marks of known makers working in such centres as London are found alone on spoons, but more commonly single marks indicate a provincial origin. The same is certainly true of Holland, and to some extent of the Scandinavian countries and Germany.

To add to the confusion, the makers of base metal spoons were not slow to realise that the public required marks of origin, and they proceeded to embellish their wares with punches which look impressive, but mean absolutely nothing as far as quality of metal is concerned. With the advent of simple plating—first the rolled plate of Sheffield, then electro-plate—the practice of stamping all sorts of marks where hallmarks ought to be gained a new lease of life, and in spite of the efforts of the authorities to see that such marks are not positively misleading, many of them continue to be so. A large number of cherished 'silver' heirlooms are actually electro-plate, while lurking among the plated spoons in the kitchen one may sometimes find an interesting silver one.

The preoccupation with marks has also led unscrupulous makers to put copies of marks pertaining to another age or country—frequently both—onto their productions; these are naturally all based on very desirable originals. It has been estimated that three times as much silver as the famous Hester Bateman made in her lifetime is now in the United States—plagiarising a saying first applied to the paintings of Corot.

All this does not mean that marks are worthless or to be disregarded. They are in fact extremely interesting and valuable, which is one good reason why no attempt is being made to introduce a sketchy table of them here—those who wish to find out about them should consult the specialist works listed in the bibliography. What really is important is to get things in the right order. Collecting spoons is interesting, and may even be profitable—but one should collect good spoons, with or without marks, not impressive marks with spoons underneath them. A real expert judges a piece of silver by its form, workmanship and patina, and, having formed an opinion, looks at the marks to see whether they confirm it. Occasionally he may be interested in the marks for themselves, just as there are collectors of signatures regardless of what they are written on, but to collect bad pictures for the signatures on them is to ask for trouble, and the same applies to spoons or any other silver.

FAKES AND FORGERIES

The demand for early spoons has been met by the production of fakes of various kinds for more than a century. Apart from genuine originals, the following varieties are in circulation—and occasionally out of circulation—in reputable museum collections:

1. Copies of early types, generally pastiches, properly marked at the time of manufacture; these, made quite without any wrongful intent, are found at all periods, and are still being made. They are particularly common from Friesland and from Norway, where they are in demand as Christening spoons.

2. Genuine early spoons, altered to make them into more desirable types; thus a George II soup spoon, with full London marks, is reshaped as a seventeenth-century

ficulate, and has an apostle or seal finial added. Occasionally a rare finial is substituted for a more common one on a completely original spoon (Fig. 10).

3. Copies made by casting, using genuine spoons as patterns; the marks are frequently very clearly reproduced (Fig. 11).

4. Copies made by the correct processes, subsequently either left unmarked (Fig. 10), or marked with punches simulating early ones (Figs. 12 and 13).

Class 1 presents no problem to those who know their hallmarks, or who consult the appropriate reference books, and Class 2 can generally be spotted by those who have studied style really carefully—although the substitution of a rare finial such as a lion sejant for the much more common seal is undetectable except by highly scientific methods, which are best left to such experts as those of Goldsmiths' Hall.

Class 3 is dangerous; modern casting technique is so good that only the most detailed examination will reveal it. Fortunately, those engaged in producing fakes are generally greedy, and make too many copies from one good original; the phenomenon of the marks on several spoons corresponding exactly in depth and spacing—something impossible to achieve when the spoons are marked separately with separate punches—is familiar to those who handle many specimens for sale, and such assemblages should be avoided. Since the practice of casting marks from genuine originals is a criminal offence under the hallmarking statutes, suspected cases in Britain should be reported to Goldsmiths' Hall.

Class 4 contains a very wide range, from the childishly bad copy to the spoon about which experts can argue without convincing one another. Fortunately, forgers are often fairly good at producing the right shapes, but tend either to use the wrong methods or, because they are out for easy money, to skimp the details and use mechanical methods of finishing, such as buffing. They are not really good art historians, and seldom combine the shape, construction, marks and engraving of a piece quite correctly—or, if they do, they get away with it.

Probably the hardest feature of an early spoon to fake is the patina of the surface. Genuine wear on a piece of silver consists partly of localised removal of metal, as on the bottom edge of a spoon, and partly of a mixture of scratches, nicks and dents produced over a long period. At every stage, the previous wear would be reduced by polishing and solution, producing a pattern of new scratches gradually shading into ancient almost obliterated ones. Silver, and especially the copper content of solder, dissolve to a considerable extent in water, and this both aids the reduction of early scars by polishing and also results in solder lines—such as those where finials are joined to stems, being etched below the level of the silver on either side. Fakers frequently use a wire brush to simulate wear, and the pattern of scratches formed in this way is easily recognisable.

The writer has produced experimental copies of early spoons which are exceedingly difficult to distinguish from originals; there is no particular reason why someone else should not do the same thing, but if he is out for a quick profit he is advised to take up some less exacting occupation.

The remedy for faking lies with the public. As long as people with inadequate knowledge are prepared to pay large sums for early pieces as investments, fakes will continue to find a market. The makers of spoons were not great artists, merely competent craftsmen, whose work can be reproduced by those who take the trouble to learn their skills. Fortunately, high standards of craftsmanship and historical scholarship seldom accompany a criminal mentality, but there have been cases in the past where very fine craftsmen have been driven to indulge in faking because there was no market for their acknowledged productions. An outstanding example is the Dutch silversmith de Haas, whose works have found their way into museums as well as into private collections; he used a wide variety of punches to apply close copies of early Dutch, Danish and other marks, some of which appear in reference books on the subject as genuine. Today, his products are belatedly being collected for their own not inconsiderable merits; perhaps some day the public will learn that the best cure for faking is a proper appreciation of contemporary craftsmanship.

NOTES

1. A wooden clamp for this purpose is in the National Museum of Antiquities of Scotland.
2. The process is well shown in an exhibit in the Nationalmuseet, Copenhagen.
3. Andreas Oldeberg: *Metallteknik Under Vikingatid Och Medeltid*, Stockholm 1966. Fig. 286 shows such a mould from Denmark.
4. Vannuccio Biringuccio: *De la Pirotechnia*, Venice 1540. New York: American Institute of Mining and Metallurgical Engineers, 1959. Translated by C. S. Smith and T. T. Gnudi.
5. For practical instructions in casting, the reader is referred to Herbert Maryon: *Metalwork and Enamelling*, London 1954, and Geoffrey Holden: *The Craft of the Silversmith*, London 1954.

Fig. 1. Three spoons of different function. *Left:* a replica of a spoon from Hoorn, 1645 (see also Fig. 102) ; has a large, round, level-edged bowl very suitable for soup, but too big to put into the mouth. *Centre:* replica of the St Ninian's Isle spoon, c. 750 (see also Fig. 38) ; has a very shallow bowl excellent for porridge, but useless for soup. *Right:* an English dessertspoon of 1792, can be used for most purposes—even soup. Replicas made by the author.

Fig. 2

Fig. 2. Three different forms of construction. *Left:* replica of a Dutch cowrie-shell bowled spoon with silver stem split to hold the shell—a difficult kind to make. *Centre:* a mother-of-pearl bowled spoon, probably Italian, c. 1650; the bowl is held in a separate piece of thin sheet silver soldered to the stem. *Right:* a modern Russian wooden spoon, carved from the solid—a survival of a very old technique, closely resembling English spoons of the fifteenth century.

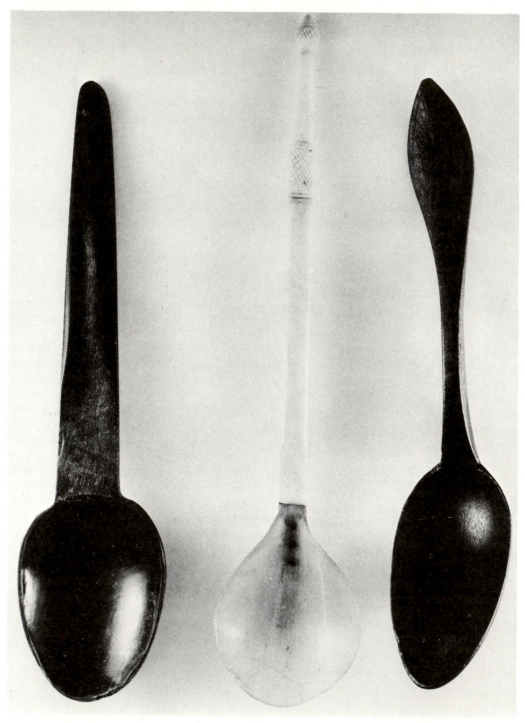

Fig. 3

Fig. 3. *Left:* a horn spoon, Scottish, nineteenth century, probably tinker made. Although a late example, this was made in exactly the same manner as the horn spoons found in occupation mounds in Friesland and elsewhere, dating from well before A.D. 1000, which were the ancestors of the flat-stemmed spoons characteristic of the Northern European plains. To make such a spoon, the horn is split and roughly shaped to outline, and is then softened by boiling and clamped in a wooden tool rather like a pair of nutcrackers to form the bowl; it may be boiled again with the clamp in position, then cooled in cold water, and finished by scraping. A groove nearly always forms along the stem, and this is clearly reproduced in many Polish and Scandinavian silver spoons of the seventeenth century (see also Figs. 68, 83 and 93). *Centre:* a modern Turkish spoon, tortoiseshell and bone, closely resembling English acorn knops of the fifteenth century, both in the bowl shape and in the finial. It is noticeable that early English acorn knops represent an ilex acorn rather than an English one, strengthening the case for regarding them as inspired by spoons from the countries invaded by the Crusaders. *Right:* wooden spoon, carved from beechwood; Danish, eighteenth century. This is of a form easy to carve in a relatively soft wood. The general shape, with pointed bowl and terminal, is found in silver spoons made all along the Baltic coast, as well as in Scotland and Ireland, in the eighteenth century.

Fig. 4. Three replicas, made by the author, illustrating evolution over four centuries. *Left:* one of five silver spoons from Iona, probably c. A.D. 1000, with shallow pointed bowls and animal's head junctions (see also Fig. 38). *Centre:* silver spoon from Rouen, c. 1300, with vestigial point to the bowl and acorn knop, as well as a fully modelled animal's head (see also Fig. 41). *Right:* a French brass spoon, probably c. 1450, in which the animal's head is replaced by the fleur-de-lys marks and the acorn is much simplified (see also Fig. 86).

Fig. 5. *Left:* spoon with cowrie-shell bowl and silver stem, made to indicate the possible origin of the Pompeian hoof ends. *Centre:* spoon made from cowrie shell, with a small silver link between the two portions; a type made in Italy in the seventeenth century, more serviceable than it looks. *Right:* another possible ancestral form, this time of the Roman *cochlearius*. All made by the author.

Fig. 6. *Left:* pattern, small moulding flask and finished finial for an apostle spoon. Normally much larger moulding flasks would be used, with several patterns, to produce a large number of finials at one pour. *Right:* replica of a Pompeian ball-knopped spoon in silver. Cast in a sand mould and finished by scraping (see also Fig. 18).

Fig. 7. From top to bottom, stages in the making of a modern nickel-silver teaspoon: the thick strip is first spread by means of tapered rollers, and the spoon blank is punched out, and stamped with a pattern between steel dies; the bowl is punched into a tin block with a steel force. A similar sequence, using hand hammers and a plain anvil, has been used since about 1660 in Britain.

Fig. 8. *Left:* replica of an Italian spoon of c. 1600. The stem is a casting, soldered to a bowl beaten out of sheet; the long tail is essential to give strength to the metal, which is softened by the soldering (see also Figs. 21, 23 and 24). *Centre:* replica of a Swiss spoon of c. 1620; the stem is hollow, formed from sheet, and the finial is a casting. This rather difficult construction did not save very much silver (see also Fig. 91). *Right:* replica of an early Flemish acorn-knop, hammered from sheet (see also Fig. 43). All made by the author.

Fig. 9. Spoons forged in the round, showing three types of junction. *Left:* as on English spoons of the fourteenth to mid-seventeenth centuries, with a short tail at the back of the bowl, formed over the edge of the anvil (see also Figs. 47 and 131). *Centre:* as on a French puritan spoon of c. 1620, with a longer tail formed by hammering into a die (see also Fig. 89). *Right:* as on some Dutch and most Scandinavian spoons, with no junction feature (see also Fig. 105). All made by the author.

Fig. 10. *Left and centre:* fakes made from George II soup spoons, the bowls reshaped and the finials added. The four marks appear together on the back of the stem, instead of one being in the bowl. This is a common (and illegal) attempted fraud. *Right:* replica of an early sixteenth-century apostle spoon, made by the author by the correct processes (including the mercury gilding of the figure): no marks, but it would need modern hallmarks to be legally saleable.

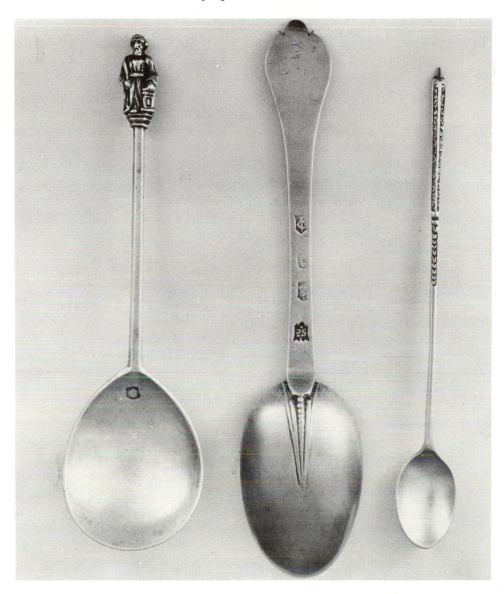

Fig. 11. *Left:* a fake made by casting, the bowl and stem from a genuine Elizabethan spoon, the finial from a pattern unknown in England; the cast marks are somewhat blurred, but quite legible. *Centre:* a very dangerous type of fake, again made by casting from a genuine original; slight blurring of the marks and absence of wear could easily pass unnoticed. *Caveat emptor! Right:* a good replica of an early Cyprus spoon, legitimately made by casting and marked 800 for 80% silver.

Fig. 12

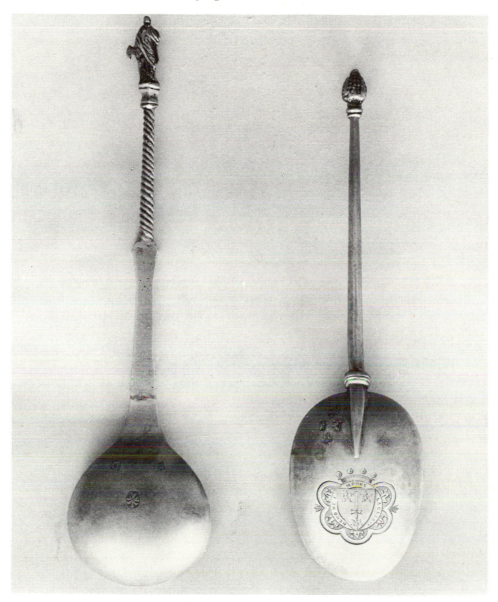

Fig. 13

Figs. 12–13. (Fig. 12 is front view, Fig. 13 back view, of same pair.) Two modern Dutch fakes. *Left:* apostle (St Matthias), the figure cast from a genuine original, the stem and bowl also cast and soldered together with a butt joint: very thick and poorly finished, with characteristic marks vaguely suggesting Bolsward. Very common, probably still in production (see also Figs. 113 and 114). *Right:* a poor copy of a Fries spoon of c. 1630, the bowl quite the wrong shape and with fake Rotterdam marks: spoons of this pattern were never made in Rotterdam (see also Fig. 100). The Scottish arms are an interesting addition.

3

The Mediterranean

SINCE the culture of Europe springs from the Near and Middle East, it would be natural to look for the earliest traces of spoons there. Unfortunately, except to a minor degree in Egypt, spoons do not appear to have played much part in the life of Middle Eastern peoples, and remains from early sites are scarce. This situation has persisted until quite recent times, and the Tuareg are apparently one of the few desert peoples to use spoons, while the majority of Indians still manage without them.

Outstanding among early finds are some small bone spoons discovered in 1961 at Catal Hayuk in Southern Anatolia.[1] These, dated from between 5700 and 5400 B.C., are of the simple functional shape common to every age: they are between 11 and 13 centimetres long, well within the range for small dessert spoons. Catal Hayuk was a food-producing community, in which every house had its grain-bins, querns and mortars: its inhabitants also used make-up, so that it is hard to tell whether the spoons were used for food or for ointment. However, they show that the idea of a spoon was familiar in the oldest civilisation yet uncovered.

EGYPT

Several millennia later than those of Catal Hayuk, the earliest Egyptian spoons also are usually of bone with shallow circular bowls and long thin stems. Several, including a tiny gold one, are known from pre-dynastic graves (before 3000 B.C.) and from their close resemblance to those made much later in Pompeii for eating eggs it seems possible that this was at least one of their uses. According to Petrie,[2] spoons are very rarely found before Greek times, when they show more variety, and are generally based on shells, with the bowls realistically modelled on recognisable species and the stems sometimes formed as arms and hands holding them. These spoons, mostly of wood or soft stone, are quite unsuitable for eating with, and are either shovels or palettes for mixing cosmetics. A possible exception is a very simple spoon from Tel el Amarna (c. 1350 B.C.) (Fig. 14) which has a bowl of cowrie shell and a plain stem, probably of silver, riveted to it: it is described as an ointment spoon, but certainly could have been used for eating. It is apparently the first of a long series of cowrie-shell bowled spoons, the material having been used in Italy and the Netherlands as late as the seventeenth century, and suggests a possible origin of the dropped-bowl design which was adapted later, first by the Greeks and then by the Romans. What appears to be a much later example is illustrated by Cabrol,[3] and has a Greek inscription on the stem.

30

Small bronze spoons, undoubtedly toilet implements, were made in Egypt in the last few centuries before Christ, and some of these appear to have influenced later Roman designs, but they do not really come within the scope of the present account. In many cases they have a short transverse bar between the stem and the bowl, giving them the outline of the crux ansata. Sir Charles Jackson[4] enlarges on this point, and suggests a general connection between spoons and sexual motifs, but in fact the majority of Egyptian spoons show no sexual imagery whatsoever, and many are severely functional.

Although spoons played, apparently, a small part in Egyptian eating habits, their design appears to have had more than a little influence on those made elsewhere. In addition to the types already mentioned, a stem formed as the head and neck of a bird, curved so that the beak points to the bowl, recurs in Roman spoons (Fig. 14).

Spoons are referred to in the Bible among the vessels of the tabernacle and of Solomon's temple,[5] but there is no mention of their use for domestic purposes, nor any indication of their shape.

Moving Westwards, we find very few spoons from Greek sites, although they become more common in the period of Roman domination. Generally of bone, they may have been a concession to the Roman fondness for eggs and snails, and shapes suitable for both have been found at Delos and at Corinth. The presumed egg-spoon has a circular bowl and a thin stem, while the other has an oval bowl and a stem sometimes flattened and decorated with circles near the bowl, followed by a tapered round part. These spoons show the marked drop from stem to bowl levels which characterises Roman patterns. It has been suggested that this may be either to facilitate resting them on a plate, or a relic of the time when spoons were made by riveting handles on to shells. The writer has experimented with this suggestion (Fig. 5), and there is no doubt that it is perfectly reasonable: whether it was actually done is another matter, and positive evidence is lacking. One point, however, soon becomes clear when one starts making copies of early spoons, and that is that the dropped-bowl design does not emerge naturally when one works in wood, bone or horn, nor is it by any means an easy one to execute in metal. The idea that it originated with a composite construction is thus eminently reasonable.

It is perhaps significant that the bowls of Greek spoons and of those from Pompeii which are culturally Greek, resemble in shape and size the shells of Cyprea Tigris, the Tiger cowrie. These shells are surprisingly tough and have glossy surfaces very suitable for eating from. They have certainly been used as spoons since the time of Akhenaten, as the specimen from Tel el Amarna shows, and were popular in Italy in the sixteenth and seventeenth centuries. In fitting a stem to such a shell, it is necessary to bend it so that it leaves the bowl almost at right angles to the plane of the rim, and this necessitates a further bend to bring it back to the normal direction. Cowrie shells vary considerably, and if one were producing a number of spoons there would be a case for separating the two bends so that the one fitting the shell could be adjusted independently of the other. The suggestion is not susceptible of proof, but is based on some experience in fitting silver mounts to cowrie shells, which can be a somewhat fiddling business (Fig. 15).

ITALY

Italian spoons have played such a notable part in the development of those made elsewhere that it is necessary to consider them as an entity.

Unfortunately the raw material, although probably plentiful, is inaccessible, undocumented for the most part and not infrequently incorrectly ascribed. Such spoons as are found tend to lurk uncared for and frequently uncleaned in museum basements and obscure corners of antique shops, the products of more than a thousand years described by the single label 'Roman—dug up in the forum'. Nevertheless, some pattern of development can be discerned, sometimes as much from what was exported as from what is found *in situ*.

The earliest known Italian spoons are Etruscan, and of these a number of complete sepcimens have survived (Fig. 16). While varying considerably in detail design, they all conform to the same general type. They are made of ivory or bone, and have pointed oval bowls of very modern outline, carried on broad stems which are often wider in the middle than near the ends: not uncommonly there is an elongated opening in the middle of the stem, or at least an engraved suggestion of one.

It is hard to say what these spoons were for. They are not entirely convincing as eating implements, although they could be used for foods such as porridge. They certainly would be unsuitable for dealing with eggs or molluscs, or anything liquid.

There is a possibility that the spoons recovered from tombs were purely ceremonial. Von Vacano,[6] quoting from (unspecified) Hittite texts, says—'(after cremation) they gather the bones with a silver spoon into a silver vessel of prescribed size which is filled with fine oil, then take them out and lay them on linen cloths—placed in the tomb'; and he suggests, from the arrangement of the tombs, that the Etruscans may have had similar ceremonies.

While interesting as a subject of study in themselves, the Etruscan spoons do not seem to have had much direct influence on later forms.

The next considerable group is that from Pompeii. As the largest, and only completely coherent, assemblage from classical times, this is of the greatest importance.

Two quite distinct types occur. The first (Fig. 19), with a shallow round bowl and a long thin stem ending in a point, bears a strong resemblance to pre-dynastic Egyptian spoons. Its purpose is made clear by a fresco (now in the Museo Nazzionale, Naples) which shows one resting across a bowl of eggs. It was a Roman superstition that it was essential to pierce the shell of an egg before opening it, to allow evil spirits to escape—hence the pointed stem.[7] It is presumably of these spoons that Martial[8] wrote:

'Sum cochleis habilis sed nec minus utilis ovis
Numquid scis potius cur cochleare vocer?'

(I am useful for shellfish but not less so for eggs
Why otherwise should I be called Cochlearius?)

These spoons were made in silver, bronze and bone, the metal ones being invariably cast in one piece and finished either on a lathe or by the use of a rotating cutter on the inside of the bowl. The stem and the upper edge of the bowl lie almost in the same plane.

Spoons of the second class have pointed oval bowls of modern shape. The stems are straight for most of their length, bending sharply down to join the bowls, under which they are continued as strengthening tails: they invariably have enlarged terminals and not pointed ends (Figs. 17 and 18).

These terminals are of two main kinds:

1. Rounded knops, occasionally ornamented as buds or balusters.
2. Pointed cloven hooves: these are sometimes realistically modelled, but more often are elongated triangles with deeply notched vertices, and there is never any attempt to model the leg of the animal. The impression conveyed, especially by the bone spoons, is of a functional rather than a purely decorative feature.

The stems of the metal spoons range from plain circular rods to hexagonal or octagonal sections ornamented with bands of moulding. The bone spoons are necessarily simpler and flatter, bowl and stem lying in one plane. All the metal spoons have been cast in one piece and finished by scraping and filing: they show no signs of hammering.

At least one possible use is suggested by the remains of porridge (made from barley) which is found on plates very similar to modern soup plates. They are quite unsuitable for dealing with eggs and doubtfully useful for molluscs, although the pointed hoof ends might be employed for extracting snails from their shells. An alternative suggestion is that they might have been designed for spearing small gobbets of meat in stews, or small fruit: they closely resemble in size and shape the small forks which are often packed with boxes of dates or crystallised fruit.

Pompeii was culturally a Greek rather than a Roman city, and it seems probable that both the diet of its inhabitants and the traditions of its craftsmen were predominantly Greek, but whether the characteristic shape of the spoons is Greek is not certainly established. Jackson illustrates a hoof-ended spoon from Cyzicus, of typically Pompeian form, as being in the British Museum, but the authorities there disclaim any knowledge of it.

Although spoons of Pompeian type are occasionally found in later assemblages, the division into two distinct varieties appears to have become blurred in the second century A.D., when both were replaced by a spoon having a fig-shaped bowl of small size, a long stem ending in a point, and a perforated junction piece between them in place of the earlier simple bend. This will be designated the Pascentia form, after the owner of one of the Mildenhall[9] examples (Figs. 15 and 20).

Spoons of this shape are found in Italy, but ironically the finest assemblages come from the northern limits of the Empire, and date from the third and fourth centuries. There are nine in the Mildenhall treasure, twenty-two from Kaiseraugst[10] and many others from elsewhere in Britain and Gaul. They were clearly in general use up to the beginning of the fifth century, and their wide dispersal had a considerable influence on the development of spoons outside Italy. The majority of the surviving examples are of silver, but enough are known of bronze to make it probable that they were originally far more common. They are invariably cast in one piece and finished by scraping rather than hammering. The bowls are often engraved, either with the chi-rho monogram or with alpha and omega, or with a presentation inscription such as the PAPPETITO VIVAS and PASCENTIA VIVAS of two of the Mildenhall spoons.

The reason for the elaboration of the junction piece, presumably from the plain form found in Greek and Pompeian spoons, is not clear. It is just possible that it is based on the finger and thumb of a hand holding the bowl, the forearm being the stem. The modelling of the junction as a hand in Egyptian spoons has already been mentioned. It is hard to see any functional value in it, and as it could not easily have been cast with the piercing in it, it represents a complication in manufacture.

Because of the sites at which many of these spoons were discovered, it is very difficult to tell how far the variations in shape were Italian or provincial in origin, but the majority appear to have been provincial. Several Gallo-Roman and Romano-British modifications are known, and these are dealt with in the appropriate place.

In addition to the Pascentia form, the Romans continued to use round-bowled spoons, as well as a variety of crux ansata outline, which would appear to have been derived from Egyptian toilet spoons (Fig. 19). Whether these were really for eating with seems doubtful, as the shape is really quite unsuitable.

Two very different kinds of spoon are found in fourth- and fifth-century hoards, mainly north of the Alps. The first, described as a ladle, had an almost hemispherical bowl and a relatively short handle: it seems probable that it was used for drinking soup.

Several were found in the treasure of the Hill of St Louis, Carthage, and are now in the British Museum. Unlike other Roman spoons, they are made in two parts, joined by soft solder, and closely resemble in outline the bronze paterae which were used for straining wine. In some, the flat junction between bowl and stem is decorated with a cross.

A very interesting variant of the form occurs in the northern part of the Empire, and is represented by five specimens from Mildenhall and one from Traprain (Fig. 20). In these the stem is formed as a well-modelled 'dolphin'—more correctly described as a coryphene fish—which in the Traprain spoon holds the bowl in its mouth. This feature, which is never found in Roman spoons from south of the Alps, appears to be of northern, possibly Scandinavian, origin; it is discussed at more length in a later chapter.

The second variety has a pear-shaped bowl, very like the Pompeian spoons, and a cylindrical stem ending in a bird's head, springing almost straight from it (Fig. 20). The stem was bent over towards the bowl, rather in the manner of modern infant feeding spoons, to form a loop. Whether this was originally symmetrical, as suggested by specimens from Canterbury,[16] or set over to one side, as in the set of fourteen from Kaiseraugst, is uncertain. It is clear that the stems were cast straight and bent afterwards, and as this could easily be done with the fingers, individual owners may have had them finished differently. A suggestion by Curle,[11] based on spoons from Traprain, that the stem was waved to fit the fingers might be true in an individual case, but not generally.

The bird's-head terminal and the absence of any junction feature represent a marked divergence from the main line of development, and suggest an independent origin. Similar spoons are known from Egypt, and it is possible that the stem is based on an ibis rather than on a swan or a duck. Some rather large spoon bowls in the Traprain treasure with fishes engraved in their centres may have been of this type, but no stems are known for them. They seem more likely to have been for serving than for eating with.

In Italy itself it is difficult to trace any survival of the Pascentia form much beyond the sixth century, to which are ascribed six from the Treasure of Isole Rizza, now in the Castelveccio, Verona. These are rather large with bobbined stems and decorated junctions, and one set of three has a Greek cross stamped in the middle of the bowl with a circular punch, with VTERE FELIX engraved about it. This appears to be the earliest instance of a stamped mark on a spoon, and is of great significance as being apparently the forerunner of bowl hallmarking.

Later developments of the Pascentia type mostly appear to be Byzantine; they are relatively plentiful and exceedingly widely dispersed, occurring in such well separated localities as Kas'r Ibrim in the Sudan and Sutton Hoo in Suffolk, where two, engraved SAULUS and PAULUS, were found in the ship burial.[12]

Byzantine spoons normally have rounded terminals and the junction between bowl and stem is formed as a solid disc. They are larger than the Roman ones, sometimes so large and heavy that one wonders what they could be used for. Many such occur in the treasures of Lampsacus and of Cyprus (British Museum); in the latter case they are ornamented in the bowls with various animals cast in low relief. They would appear to be serving spoons, and may be compared with the tablespoons with heavily embossed bowls which have been made (frequently from plain Georgian spoons) intermittently for the past century—primarily as wedding presents.

All these Byzantine spoons, like their predecessors, were cast in one piece. This method of construction is, to a modern craftsman, so difficult that one wonders why it was adopted. This is because modern casting is commonly done into split sand moulds, in which the chilling effect of the moist sand and the gases produced when it is suddenly heated combine to prevent the metal from running into the thinner parts. The writer has succeeded, with considerable trouble, in casting replicas of the simpler Pompeian spoons into sand, but the process is very uncertain.

Sand moulding was unknown until the fourteenth century, earlier work being generally cast in baked clay moulds: these were heated before the metal was poured, and allowed of much thinner sections being produced. An excellent contemporary account of the process, as used in a brass foundry in Milan about 1430, is given in Chapter 8 of Biringuccio's Pirotechnia.[13]

The work involved in finishing spoons cast in this way was relatively small, and did not require the removal of much material. Casting was a natural method of handling metal to craftsmen brought up largely to use bronze and lacking modern facilities for machining. The tradition has persisted, and recent examples of silver spoons cast in one piece are found from Southern Italy and Egypt.

Capua, which is only about thirty miles from Pompeii, was the principal bronze working town in the Empire, and it is possible that much of the bronze found in Pompeii was made there, while Alexandria on the other hand maintained an important output of silver. It seems probable that craft traditions established in these centres have been maintained since before the beginning of our era, surviving the political and religious upheavals of two thousand years.

Unlike the Pascentia spoon, the Pompeian porridge spoon had a number of obvious descendants. These are almost impossible to date individually, but can be placed in what appear to be two coherent evolutionary series.

In the first of these, which will be called series A, the oval bowl, relatively short stem, sharp drop from stem to bowl, and enlarged terminal of the Pompeian spoons are retained throughout (Figs. 21 and 25). Variations are limited to the ornamentation of the stem and the shape of the terminal, which goes through a number of transformations without ever becoming completely unrecognisable. In the limits of these transformations are found volute ends, half-female figures, flattened rectangular plates rather like small spades, and seal tops; but a large number of intermediate forms link these always back to the original hoof, than which there is no more persistent feature of spoon design.

A particularly interesting finial, on a spoon in the Victoria and Albert Museum, has the stem cut off obliquely and upswept. The derivation from the hoof is quite apparent, but so is the resemblance to the slip end which is found later on French and English spoons. It would thus appear that the slip end is really a limiting form of the hoof (Fig. 26).

Silver spoons of this series are found with marks up to the early eighteenth century, and can be dated with some confidence. Renaissance and later examples have the bowl and stem made as separate pieces soldered together, but similar spoons in bronze are cast in one piece. This is understandable in view of the very different characteristics of the two metals, and the need for economy in finishing silver.

Italian hoof-ended spoons made a sudden impact on northern Europe early in the seventeenth century. They were copied extensively in Holland, where they rapidly evolved into characteristic Dutch forms, but found little favour in England, and none in Scandinavia.

A variant of the basically Pompeian form has a twisted upper stem, sometimes rounded at the end and sometimes ending in a clenched fist (Figs. 27, 28 and 29). It is of interest as being the probable ancestor of the twisted-stem spoons which were popular in southern Germany in the second half of the seventeenth century, and somewhat later in Russia. The clenched fist terminal is also found in Copenhagen, one of the few apparent instances of Italian influence in Denmark, although the possibility of completely independent development must also be considered.

A feature which is absent from the first-century spoons, but which occurs frequently thereafter, is a barb moulded on the lower part of the stem, giving the effect of a tang on the bowl having been driven into a socket. The combination of this feature with a volute terminal, particularly common in Southern Italy, so closely resembles a small bone—as from a chicken—as to suggest that it might have been modelled from one, but the barb is found indiscriminately with all forms of finial. It is reproduced in the earliest Dutch hoof ends, and survives in the fiddle pattern and derived styles of more recent times. Whether it represents an original constructional feature is a matter for conjecture.

The second evolutionary series, series B, proceeded through a lengthening of the stem, rounding of the bowl, and virtual elimination of the drop between the two, to a spoon of quite different appearance. Which of the three principal variants is the earliest is almost impossible to establish; they comprise:

1. Silver spoons with round bowls, twisted stems and perforated finials; several of these, found in Cyprus, have the lion of St Mark stamped below a cross in the bowl, and are presumed to be Venetian work of the fifteenth century. They have crowned masks soldered halfway down the stems, possibly as an aid to use (Fig. 30).

These spoons show several anomalous features. The bowls are quite round, which is very rare in Italy; the twisted stem, with the short flattened portion linking it to the bowl, and the central mask, are not found in other Italian spoons, and the terminals show no connection with earlier types. There is a striking resemblance between these spoons and those made in Bergen in the early seventeenth century, and it seems possible that both may have been derived from a pattern made somewhere in Central Europe.

2. Bronze or brass spoons with slightly oval bowls, narrow flattened beaded stems and oval terminals, generally with at least a suggestion of a hoof motif. The beading was formed by hammering into a die, and the whole spoon was probably made from sheet. There is almost invariably a mark in the bowl in a circle of pellets, occasionally a cross but often clearly something else (Fig. 31). These spoons are found right across northern Italy; one specimen, in the Vatican Museum, is labelled 'C. IV–V, from the catacombs', but this dating is quite inconsistent with other evidence.

3. Bronze spoons very similar in outline to (2), but with flattened polygonal stems and clearly formed hoof terminals; they were cast in one piece, and frequently have a roughened grip chased on the lower stem and single makers' marks in the bowls (Fig. 22). The distribution is the same as (2), but they are less common. Types (2) and (3) are very clearly related, and may represent a compromise between the traditional Pompeian form and round-bowled spoons derived from further north. A spoon of this type is clearly shown in a picture 'Esau selling his birthright' by Luca Giordano (1632–1705) —now in Perth City Museum.

It seems likely that most of the brass and bronze spoons were gilt; surviving examples are usually in poor condition and difficult to examine or photograph clearly. Unlike other Italian spoons, they do not appear to be represented at all in the museums of northern Europe, and so have not attracted the attention they deserve—as the apparent ancestors, through the trefids, of all modern shapes.

The placing of the marks in the bowl, particularly the twin marks of the Venice spoons, provides a link between the Chi-Rho monogram of late Roman cochlearii, through the stamped cross of the Isole Rizza spoons, to the bowl marks which were used on all English spoons made before 1660, the Cyprus spoons of the Kingdom of Jerusalem period and the rare bowl-marked Dutch spoons of the early seventeenth century. There can be little doubt that the practice originated in Italy, probably in the Veneto, and certainly before the fourteenth century.

The remaining group of spoons in Italy is of far-reaching importance. Comprising those with fig-shaped bowls, thin polygonal stems and small knops, it is one to which so many other European spoons, including virtually all English ones made between the end of the Hundred Years' War and the Restoration, belong. To avoid any geographical or cultural implications, this group will be referred to as ficulates (Fig. 33).

In plan they are not unlike the Roman cochlearii, but the side view is very different: instead of the bowl being set well below the stem, with an intermediate junction piece, it springs directly from it, curving gracefully down from the shoulder to an almost crescentic outline. Such spoons were generally made, not by casting, but by forging from relatively thick blanks—in fact a good starting point is a round bar about 1 centimetre in diameter and 5–7 centimetres long. They are called 'cones' and 'finials' by Hilton Price[14] and, made of brass (sometimes referred to as latten) or bronze, are common all over western Europe. Several minor variations occur: these affect principally the knop, which may be an acorn, a small baluster-end, a small knob with spiral grooving (wrythen-knop), a small conical affair rather like a bud, or simply an obliquely cut-off end (slip end); significantly, it is hardly ever a hoof. There are also variations in the bowl shape, and a very few specimens have round and level-edged bowls on polygonal stems: these are not strictly speaking ficulates, but may represent an early transitional form linking true ficulates to the early round-bowled spoons of the Northern assemblage. They are rare, and may not be Italian at all.

Some base metal ficulate spoons are very light and rather crudely made, but the best compare favourably with other kinds. Many of these superior specimens bear marks struck on the back of the bowl, close to the stem—usually of Lombardic letters in shaped outlines, and apparently never in circles of pellets. It seems probable that these spoons were mostly gilt all over, but some may have been tinned.

Silver ficulate spoons are exceedingly rare in Italy, if they exist at all, but a seal top from Dubrovnik (Fig. 26), dated by C. C. Oman[15] close to 1300, is of the form. The top of the seal is not circular, but markedly elongated from front to back, and somewhat sloping: it may be a development of the hoof end, a suggestion borne out by the faintly hoof-like aspect of some early English seal tops.

An almost identical seal terminal is found on a silver spoon, with the typical Italian oval bowl, in the Haagsgemeentemuseum.

Silver ficulate spoons of apparently very early date are found in Cyprus: their form led at one time to their being described as English, but the researches of Mr Oman have established that the marks pertain to the Kingdom of Jerusalem, established in 1191 by Richard Coeur-de-Lion (Fig. 30). Most have acorn finials, but one, now in the Victoria and Albert Museum, has a well-modelled female head and bust.

The question of the origin of these spoons, and of their relationship to those of England and France, is left to be discussed at a later stage.

Something must be said of the forks which, from the Renaissance onwards, so often accompany Italian spoons. The possible use of the hoof end on some Pompeian spoons has already been mentioned. It would be logical to expect the next development to be a combined implement, or sucket fork, but none is known from Italy—although the two specimens from Sevington, described in the next section, are presumably not the only ones to have been made in the early middle ages.

Such Italian forks as appear to be early are mostly made to match the lozenge and volute-end spoons of Pompeian form, but one with a stem to match a ficulate slip end is in the museum at Padua.

Although the use of two-pronged forks has occasionally been ascribed to the Romans, neither literature nor specimens confirm the suggestion. The late Roman equivalent appears to have been an implement with one curved prong, of which examples are known from St Ninian's Isle, Canterbury and Kaiseraugst,[16] but not apparently from Italy. In spite of a suggestion made (in connection with the St Ninian's Isle specimen)[17] that the purpose was the cutting and division of Communion wafers, it is now quite clear that these were eating implements. They would have served very well for prising molluscs out of their shells, and might also have been used for picking up small pieces of fruit or even meat. For such purposes the curved prong would serve much better than the straight tip of a cochlearius.

The first mention of a true fork occurs about 1000,[18] when a Byzantine princess married to the son of Doge Pietro Orseolo incurred the strictures of St Peter Damien for using one—in terms which do not suggest that it was common practice in the Venice of the time. Forks are next mentioned again in Florence in 1361, in the list of plate belonging to the Commune:[19] this contains twenty knives, forty spoons and forty-three forks. From this time on forks are common, frequently in pairs with spoons.

Nothing has been said of the highly decorated spoons, with bowls of rock crystal, agate, or cowrie shell and elaborate gold or silver mounts, of which many survive from the fifteenth and sixteenth centuries. These conform in general to the simpler groups, but, being individual works of art, cannot be adequately dealt with in a general account.

One type does deserve mention, being relatively common. This has the bowl and stem made from a shell of Cyprea mediterranea, joined by a small silver link riveted to both portions (Fig. 5). These spoons appear very flimsy, but Cyprea shells are surprisingly tough, and maintain a highly polished surface in use. The writer has had a replica of one of these spoons in daily use for over five years and it shows no signs of wear or damage, so the type may have been practicable as well as economical of silver (Fig. 5).

In what can be discerned from the material available, there is nothing to suggest that the successive waves of barbarian invaders which overcame Italy from the fifth century onwards had any influence on the design of spoons. Apart from the ficulates, whose origin is discussed later, all the types found up to the seventeenth century can be traced to those known in the first, and, except in the Venetian silver spoons, motifs characteristic of the northern countries appear to be conspicuously absent. The few spoons of entirely foreign aspect which are found appear to be imported.

SPAIN

Very little work has been done on the spoons of Spain.[20] The majority were probably made of wood, box and juniper being particularly favoured. Such few silver spoons as have come to the writer's notice strongly resemble Italian ones. Their scarcity is generally blamed on the Napoleonic wars, but it is possible that they are not really so scarce as appears, but simply have not aroused much interest among collectors and museum authorities.

NOTES

1. *Illustrated London News*, 9 June 1962, page 936.

2. Sir W. M. Flinders Petrie: *Social Life in Ancient Egypt*, London 1923, page 101.

3. F. Cabrol and H. Leclerq: *Dictionnaire d'Archéologie Chrétienne et de Liturgie*, Paris 15 vols. 1907–53, page 3180.

4. Sir Charles Jackson: *Illustrated History of English Plate*, London 1911.

5. Exodus 37, Numbers 7.

6. Otto Wilhelm von Vacano: *The Etruscans in the Ancient World*, London 1960, translated by S. A. Ogilvie.

7. See Pliny's *Natural History*, Book XXVIII.

8. Martial, Book XIV, 121.

9. British Museum: The Mildenhall Treasure: Provisional Handbook 1947, item nos. 27 and 28. Also D. E. Strong: *Greek and Roman Gold and Silver Plate*, London 1966.

10. *The Times*, London, 8 February 1966.

11. A. O. Curle: *The Treasure of Traprain*, Glasgow 1923.

12. British Museum: *The Sutton Hoo Ship Burial*, 1947, Plate 16.

13. Biringuccio: *De la Pirotechnia*, Book 1.

14. F. G. Hilton Price: *Old Base Metal Spoons*, London 1908.

15. Private communication.

16. *Illustrated London News*, 14 July 1962. See also catalogue of the Römermuseum, 1963.

17. A. C. O'Dell: The St Ninian's Isle Treasure. *Antiquity*, XXXIII, page 241.

18. Quoted from the catalogue of an exhibition in Bologna: Salone Internazionale dell'Alimentazione Mostra della Posateria Moderna e Antica, 8–22 May 1958—'ella si faceva trinciare le vivande in minute pezzi che poi portava alla bocca con certo forchetto d'oro a due rebbi . . . un lusso insensato che richiamo la collera celeste su di lei e sul marito.' Both died of the plague.

19. Ibid.

20. Luis Monreal Tejada: *Biografía de Lasopa la Escudilla y la Cuchara. Historia y Vida*, April 1972, No. 49. D. E. Strong: *Greek and Roman Gold and Silver Plate*, London 1966.

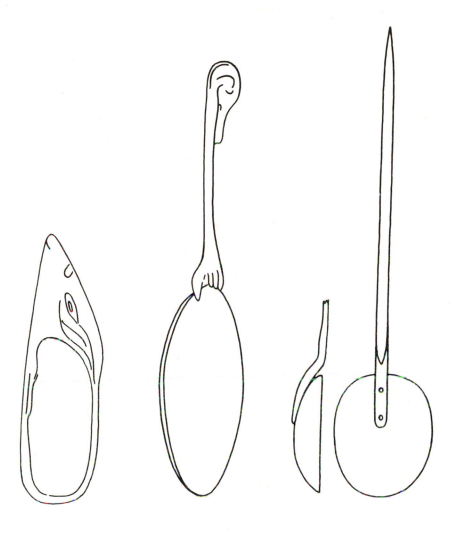

Fig. 14. Egyptian spoons. *Left:* ivory, probably a palette for mixing cosmetics, 1310–1200 B.C Fitzwilliam Museum, Cambridge. *Centre:* ivory with duck (or ibis) terminal, age not known. *Right:* with cowrie shell bowl and silver stem, from Tel el Amarna, c. 1350 B.C. The Louvre.

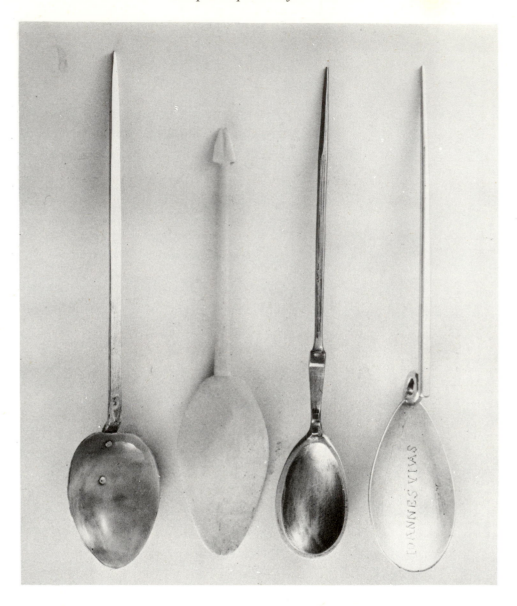

Fig. 15. Four replicas made by the author to test possible uses of spoons. *Left:* of a spoon from Tel el Amarna, c. 1350 B.C. *Left centre:* of a bone spoon from Pompeii. *Right centre:* of a Roman spoon, c. A.D. 300. *Right:* of a Roman spoon from Mildenhall, c. A.D. 400.

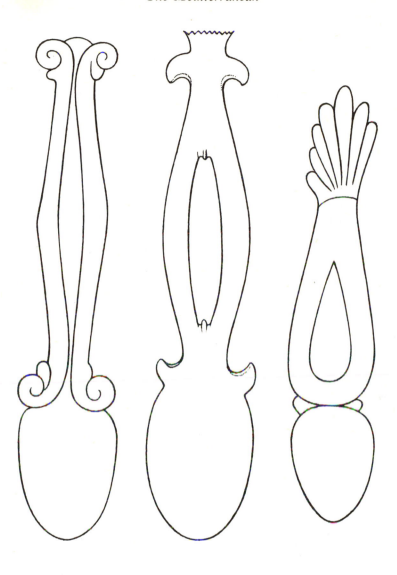

Fig. 16. Three Etruscan ivory spoons. Those in the middle and on the right have openings in the centre. Length of left-hand spoon 18 cm. British Museum.

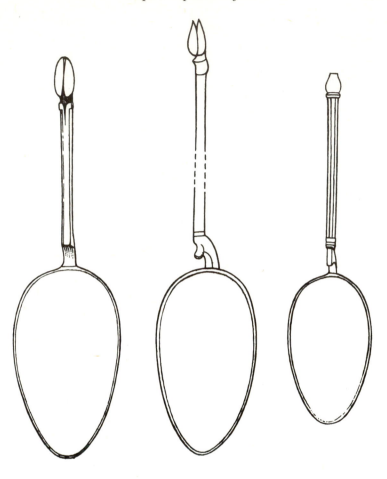

Fig. 17. Three silver spoons from Pompeii. *Left:* with hoof terminal closely foreshadowing an Italian variety common in the seventeenth century. Length 14 cm. British Museum. *Centre:* with more cloven hoof. Length 15·3 cm. *Right:* with hexagonal stem and bud finial. Length 12·4 cm. Pompeii Museum.

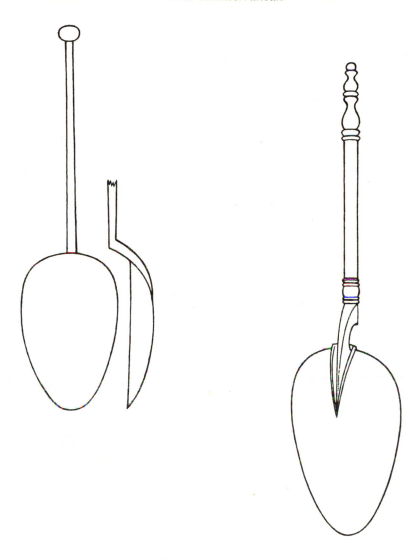

Fig. 18. Two more silver spoons from Pompeii. *Left:* with circular stem and ball knop. *Right:* with moulded stem and bobbin finial. Length 16·6 cm. Pompeii Museum.

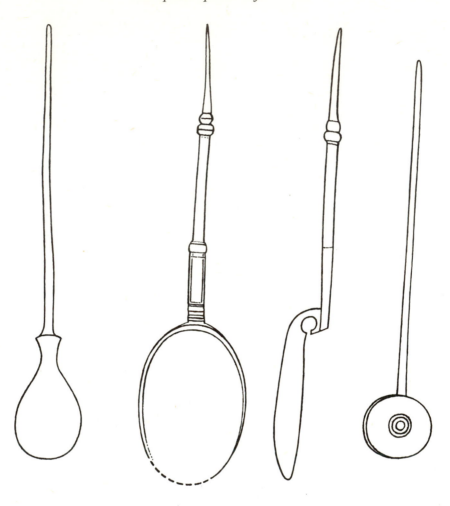

Fig. 19. Roman spoons. *Left:* of *crux ansata* form, c. A.D. 200; a type found in bronze and silver. *Centre* (front and side views): from Benwell Fort on Hadrian's Wall, silver, fourth century. Newcastle University Museum of Archaeology. *Right:* with circular bowl finished in a lathe. Pompeii Museum.

Fig. 20. Three late Roman silver spoons, possibly made in Britain or Gaul. *Left:* with duck's head terminal, the stem originally curved back over the bowl. *Centre:* the normal form, with pointed stem and pear-shaped bowl, engraved with the Chi Rho monogram. *Right:* dolphin ladle, cast in one piece and finished in the bowl by turning in a lathe. All from Traprain Law. National Museum of Antiquities of Scotland.

Fig. 21. Spoon and fork, maker's mark GP. Length of spoon 15·5 cm., weight 36 grams. Marks for Padua, seventeenth century. The form is derived from the Pompeian hoof ends. The central moulding is a common feature of Italian spoons.

Fig. 22. *Left:* bronze hoof end spoon, marked in the bowl, probably originally gilt. Age uncertain, possibly fifteenth century. *Centre:* bronze fork with female figure terminal, Italian, seventeenth century. *Right:* gilt bronze spoon, Italian, seventeenth century Length 15·2 cm.

Fig. 23. *Left and centre:* fork and spoon with volute terminals, matching, but by different makers, Naples 1714. *Right:* lozenge-end fork, unmarked, of very base silver. Italian, early seventeenth century. Length of spoon 13·7 cm., weight 22 grams.

Fig. 24. Lozenge-end spoon of typical seventeenth-century form, Spoleto. Length 15·5 cm.
Messrs Bulgari.

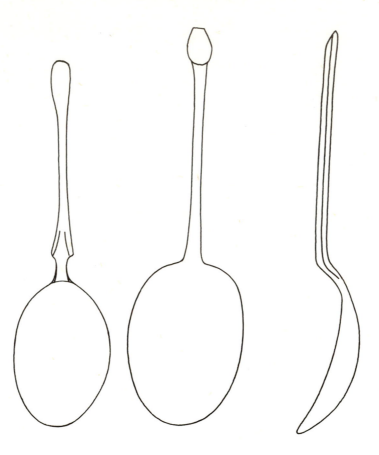

Fig. 25. Three cast bronze Italian spoons, of forms common in the north of the country. All probably seventeenth century. Length of centre spoon 14 cm.

Fig. 26. *Left:* silver spoon with unswept slip end, apparently derived from a hoof terminal. Unmarked, possibly sixteenth century. *Centre and right* (front and side views) : Italianate seal top, showing derivation from a hoof end. Engraved with the crest of a Dubrovnik family, probably fourteenth century. Victoria and Albert Museum.

Fig. 27

Figs. 27–28 (front and back views of same pair). *Left:* spoon with clenched fist terminal, mark MB on the finial. Dated 1670, engraved with a marriage coat of arms of somewhat Germanic aspect. Italian, probably Rome, c. 1670. Length 15·7 cm., weight 52 grams. *Right:* a lighter spoon of similar outline, later French import marks only. Probably Italian, but possibly Spanish, c. 1680. Length 16·5 cm., weight 32 grams.

Fig. 29. Front and back views of cast bronze spoon with twist stem. Italian, mid seventeenth century. Dug up near Lake Iseo, with a hoof end spoon and a bronze plate.

Fig. 30. Two early spoons dug up in Cyprus, now in the Museum at Nicosia. *Left:* acorn knop with bowl mark for Famagusta (a lion), showing the characteristic narrow angle at the shoulder and four-sided stem. *Right:* spoon with the lion of St Mark for Venice punched below a cross. Both probably fourteenth century. Cyprus Government photographs.

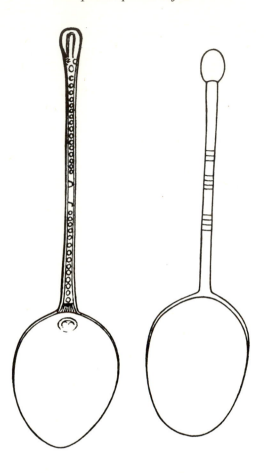

Fig. 31. Two derivatives of the hoof end, both brass or bronze. *Left:* with beaded stem, marked in the bowl with a device which is sometimes a cross, common in the Veneto. Length 15 cm. *Right:* with plain disc end, unmarked. Both probably seventeenth century, but some examples may be earlier.

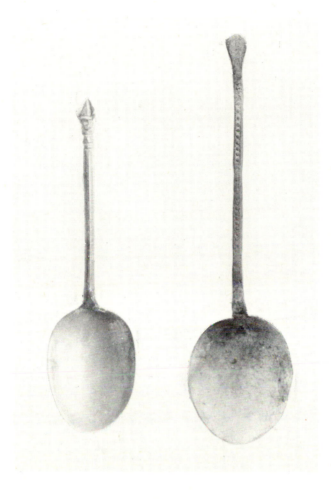

Fig. 32. *Left:* pointed hoof end spoon, bronze, cast in one piece, Venice. *Right:* beaded stem spoon with bowl mark, brass or bronze; the marks, which range from a cross to makers' initials, are almost invariably punched in a pelleted circle. Brescia, Museo e Pinacoteca.

Fig. 33. Three Italian bronze or brass spoons, all probably fourteenth or fifteenth century, and of the early ficulate pattern which, it is suggested, was the inspiration of English and French spoons. They are of the type described by Hilton Price as 'cones' and 'finials'. The two on the left are marked on the back of the bowl and have certainly been gilt all over. That on the right is unmarked, and any gilding has disappeared. Length of centre spoon 16 cm.

4

Northern Europe

THERE is very little evidence of the use of spoons in non-Mediterranean Europe before the coming of the Romans. Probably the earliest are those from the late Neolithic complex of Vinča, near Belgrade; made of bone, they resemble stumpy oars, and show clear signs of wear in use. The people of Vinča came from the Middle East, but there is no evidence whether they brought the use of spoons with them or evolved it on the spot.

Somewhat later are some wooden spoons or ladles, carved in the shape of ducks, from the peat bog of Gorbundovo[1] in the central Urals. These are interesting, because the use of shapes based on ducks or swans has persisted over a very long period, and is found in the Russian kovsh.

A few pottery spoons[2] are known from Neolithic sites, both in England and on the Continent. They are crude, and appear to have been cooking rather than eating implements. Sporadic occurrences of spoons in other prehistoric sites are known, but they are insufficient even to establish their general use, let alone give any indication of stylistic trends.

A number of bronze scoops[3] have been found in Iron Age graves on both sides of the Channel. They occur normally in pairs, one with a cross in the bowl and the other perforated near one edge, and are presumed to be for some kind of ritual. The cross is certainly not a Christian emblem. It is possible that the use is related to that of some round-bowled strainer spoons which are found, with crystal balls mounted in strapwork, in the graves of Jutish ladies at a much later period (Fig. 35). It has been suggested that they were for the straining and testing of wine. The tradition that a crystal ball went cloudy in poisoned wine must, if taken literally, have led to a number of untimely deaths. The shape of these strainers is quite different from that of the bronze scoops, being quite possibly derived from Roman paterae or from the rare round-bowled late Roman period spoons such as those from Carthage and Desana.[4]

Negative evidence is always unsatisfactory. It is quite possible that the people inhabiting northern and central Europe before the time of Caesar habitually used wooden or horn spoons to eat their porridge with, and that none of these have been preserved. What does appear reasonably certain is that they did not use their precious supply of metal to make them from. This is entirely understandable, as gold and silver were too scarce and bronze, unless gilt or tinned, is not pleasant to eat from. It was only with the coming of the legions that spoons began to be a consistent feature of domestic assemblages, and then probably only in the homes of Romans or Romanised natives.

Roman spoons of types already discussed in the last chapter have been found at many sites in northern Europe—notably at Mildenhall, Traprain Law, and in the Rhineland from Cologne to Kaiseraugst. In addition to the normal forms, a large number of minor variations are recognisable.[5] Unfortunately, the sporadic occurrence and subsequent dispersal of these makes it very difficult to detect definite provincial trends. One of the spoons from Mildenhall (Pappetito's) is sufficiently different from the others to suggest that it was made in a different part of the Empire, since the difference in age between Pappetito and her sister Pascentia was presumably not great. Three silver spoons from Foxcote in Suffolk (in the Cambridge University Museum of Archaeology—Fig. 34) have a very small drop from stem to bowl, with a simple bend in place of the usual pierced junction, and these could well be of local origin; the outline closely resembles that of the Barham Down spoon described later. Some spoons in the museum at Bonn have finials which closely resemble the balusters, seals and slip ends made in England in the sixteenth century, but there is nothing to suggest a link between the two groups.

A very few folding spoons, all of bronze, are known from sites in Britain, such as Traprain Law, Wroxeter and Chesterton.

Some rather primitive bone spoons, including a few with perforated bowls, have been found in forts along Hadrian's wall: their purpose is obscure.

With the withdrawal of the Roman garrisons, the supply of imported Roman spoons dried up, but local variants of them were probably made sporadically for some years. One of the most interesting of these is the Barham Down spoon, which is a decorated example of the simplified cochlearius found at Foxcote (Fig. 36). Its present whereabouts are unknown, and the copy in the Victoria and Albert museum is clearly inaccurate, but fortunately good illustrations[6] are available. The lower part of the stem is modelled as a bird, whose beak holds the upper part and whose legs trail under the bowl: it has no body or wings, but a small fan-shaped ornament in the bowl apparently represents its tail. The main part of the stem is round and parallel, with four sets of reeding, and the finial represents a curious long-legged crouching beast which is probably a lion. Although derived from the Roman pattern, this spoon is unlike any known Roman work: the ornament suggests Scandinavian influence, but it is possible that it was made in England. Dating is conjectural, but it is unlikely to be later than the sixth century. A spoon from Desborough illustrated on the same plate has a much simpler outline, with a somewhat broader bowl, a round stem with simple step down at the bowl and a flattened terminal pierced with a round hole. The terminal alone distinguishes it from true Roman patterns, but it is clearly in the Roman tradition, and is probably of similar age to the Barham Down spoon.

Most of the spoons so far described in this chapter show clear affinities with Roman ones: those which follow represent the beginnings of a new tradition.

Possibly the earliest is that from the St Ninian's treasure (Fig. 38), found associated with numerous silver bowls and other articles and a single-pronged fork. This has a very shallow leaf-shaped bowl and a long thin stem, with the cast head of a dog (with blue glass eyes) riveted over the junction.

In the original account of the find,[7] it was suggested that the one-pronged fork was for cutting, and the spoon for dispensing, Communion wafers, and indeed that the whole hoard was ecclesiastical: this opinion seems to have hardened into legend.[8] The first surmise is completely contradicted by the specimens found elsewhere, and the suggestion that the spoon could not have been used for ordinary domestic purposes (a suggestion previously made in connection with the Iona spoons presently to be described) is discounted by experiments with replicas, which prove perfectly serviceable. The St Ninian's spoon, being of silver, is perhaps not fully representative of its period, but that it was intended for any purpose except eating food cannot be regarded as established. Exactly where and when it was made remains a mystery.

Of slightly later date are the two unfinished combined spoons and forks from a hoard of coins and silver scrap dug up at Sevington in Wiltshire and dated about A.D. 850 (Figs. 37, 38). These are blanks cast to shape and marked out for finishing: the maker has started at the fork end of one, broken a tine near the root, and then broken the blank in half for melting, while the other has not been hammered at all. What is particularly interesting about these two, apart from the earliest appearance of a definite two-pronged fork, is the animals' heads which occur at each end of the flat portions of the stem, and which clearly indicate an early use of this motif.

Basically similar in design, the five spoons from Iona[9] (Fig. 38) and one each from Pevensey,[10] Taunton and Ribe[11] (Fig. 39) all have animals' head junctions between bowl and stem and shallow bowls decorated with engraving. The attribution of the Iona spoons to the twelfth century and to France appears, in the light of the Sevington specimens, improbable, and they may well all be pre-conquest Saxon work. The general shape agrees closely with that of some undated bone spoons from Norway[11] and London (Fig. 39).

The ornament on the stem of the best of the Iona spoons suggests waves, through which the owner of the head is swimming—so presumably it is a fish or sea monster. Distinctly fishy outlines and motifs recur in northern European spoons until the seventeenth century, as in the scale pattern which decorates many Groningen examples.

That the leaf-shaped bowl was in general use is confirmed by a number of other apparently early fragments (Fig. 35), as well as by the presence of a vestigial point to the bowl in spoons made somewhat later.

An entirely different style is shown by a group of spoons, all apparently early fourteenth century, which includes four from Rouen (Victoria and Albert Museum), one each from Brechin, Windymains Water and Montrose (National Museum of Antiquities of Scotland) and some others of unknown provenance (Figs. 41 to 43). In all of these the bowl is nearly circular, with a level edge, and the stem thin and straight with a simple acorn or diamond finial. In two of the Rouen spoons the junction is ornamented with a sea-monster's head, and these have the Rouen town mark in the bowl. They resemble very closely silver and horn spoons from Sweden (described by Ugglas)[12] (Figs. 40 and 44) which are apparently eleventh or twelfth century.

Numerous spoons of generally similar aspect exist as isolated finds, generally without any recorded provenance. They are sufficiently clearly differentiated from the earlier leaf-ended and the later ficulate spoons to constitute a definite class, having features in common with both groups.

A few, such as an elegant diamond-pointed spoon from Dijon (Fig. 46), are hard to fit into any category, but probably belong to the same period. Apart from these the evidence all suggests that, up to the middle of the fourteenth century, the round-bowled spoon was in general use in northern Europe.

An abrupt change, comparable with that produced in England in 1660 by the restoration of Charles II, occurred during the ensuing half-century. The round-bowled spoons disappeared and were replaced by ficulates, differing not only in bowl shape but in the basic process of manufacture. That it was no gentle evolution is shown by the fact that all the early spoons of this kind show an acute angle at the end of the bowl against the stem and have elongated bowls with strongly curved profiles. A gradual reversion towards a more rounded and level-edged bowl occurred during the succeeding two centuries.

The suggestion has already been made that the origin of the ficulate pattern in Italy could be traced to the eastern Mediterranean, possibly through Cyprus. Whether the style came to Britain and France directly from the Crusader settlements, or through Italy, is probably not ascertainable, but certain Italian features common in very early English ficulate spoons suggest the latter. Attention is called to some of these in the descriptions accompanying plates of individual spoons.

By A.D. 1450 the fully-developed ficulate spoon was established as the general form in silver both in England and in France (Figs. 47, 48 and 87), and the next two centuries saw only relatively minor variations of it. The makers of brass spoons were probably rather more conservative, and round-bowled examples are found as late as the last quarter of the seventeenth century.

The ficulate revolution did not reach the Netherlands until much later, and Scandinavia until later still: here short-stemmed, round-bowled spoons were made in silver well into the seventeenth century, and in Sweden into the eighteenth, and the ficulate never became the dominant form.

In museum and private collections alike, spoons of silver have pride of place. This can lead one to forget that over most of Europe the great bulk of the population probably never even saw a silver spoon, but ate from horn or wood. Such humble implements were seldom preserved, and so early examples are now much rarer than those of silver. There is, however, abundant evidence that designs in silver were repeatedly drawn from those in other materials. In particular, the shape which comes most naturally in horn, and which was being made for general use in Scotland until very recently, is the parent of seventeenth-century spoons in the belt of country bordered by the southern shores of the Baltic and the North Sea. Many of these reproduce not only the general outline, but the groove in the upper side of the stem which represents the original inside of the horn.

In the forested regions a little further south, wood was the general material, and the rather stumpy spoons made from burrs of maple and other close-grained wood led in due course to equally stumpy metal ones. Since shells suitable for spoon bowls were not readily available, it is natural that forms based on shells are absent until a much later date.

The persistence of the animals' head junction, which must be regarded as the main contribution of northern Europe to spoon decoration, reflects the fondness of the northern peoples for zoomorphic ornament (Figs. 38–45, 62, 66 and 113). Just as the numerous derivatives of the hoof terminal indicate Italian influence, so the animal's head shows influence from north of the Alps. The two are never seen together—a fact which, in view of the many hybrids which do occur, is a little surprising.

To sum up, it does appear as though three distinct ancestral forms contribute to the diverse kinds of European spoon which are found after the Renaissance, viz—

(i) Cast hoof ends. The origin of these, which have contributed so much to so many descendants, cannot be traced back beyond Graeco-Roman culture of about 200 B.C., but is believed to have been a handled shell like that from Tel el Amarna.

(ii) Round-bowled spoons, nearly always with animal's head junctions. The earliest occurrence of the form is in the dolphin ladles, generally classed as Roman, but more probably originating well north of the Alps. The very few such spoons from Mediterranean sites are likely to be intrusive. The Desana[4] spoons, the later Jutish strainers and the spoons from Sigtuna and Gotland[11] all belong to this group, as do the Rouen spoons and those made in the Netherlands and Germany until the end of the seventeenth century. The originals were probably of horn, and designed for use with liquids.

(iii) Ficulate spoons. Although some early oar-shaped bone spoons with animal's head junctions are known from Norway and Britain, the writer is inclined to place the origin of the ficulate form in the Near East, and to regard its spread to Western Europe as being one of the many cultural legacies of the Crusades. The first appearance of the type seems to follow the eviction of the Crusaders and their families from Palestine after their defeat at the Horns of Hattin in 1187. There are good historical parallels for the suggested adoption of an article from an occupied country in this way—to mention a few, tobacco pipes from North America, curry from India and anoraks from the Arctic. A part of the world which introduced the Crusading armies to sugar, maize, melons and lemons, and enlarged their vocabulary by such words as marmalade, sofa and pussy-cat could equally easily have influenced their ideas on spoons.

This hypothesis is supported by the fact that spoons made in Egypt and Turkey well into this century are surprisingly similar to English ones of the late middle ages. Not only are the bowls the same shape, but many of these spoons have acorn finials, clearly based on the evergreen oak which is common in the wooded parts of Asia Minor and Syria. The acorns on early English spoons are far more like these than those found on English oaks. A further significant fact, mentioned earlier on, is that the first Western ficulate spoons have the narrow bowls, with acute angles where they join the stems, which are found in an extreme form in the spoons made in Cyprus in the period of the Kingdom of Jerusalem.

Differences in derivation of the different forms of spoon are suggested by etymology. *Cucciaio* in Italy and *cuilliere* in France derive from the Latin *cochlearius* and indicate a connection with shells—although, with all due deference to Martial, it seems questionable whether it is because they were used for eating things found in shells, or because they were originally made from them. In the North, *ske* in Scandinavian languages and *spoon* in Anglo-Saxon both signify a piece of wood, and clearly refer to material. *Ladle*, *lepel* (Dutch), *löffel* (German) and *lozzka* (Russian) all appear to be from the same root, and to signify an article held to the lips, that is, a soup spoon. It is very noticeable that spoons so described are generally too big to be put right into the mouth.

Although the word for a spoon, once established in any language, is applied to all varieties, it is clear that *spoon* and *ske* were originally used to designate shallow, pointed-bowl implements of the St Ninian's and Iona types.

NOTES

1. A. L. Mongait: *Archaeology in the USSR*, Harmondsworth 1961, Plate 3b.
2. Stuart Piggott: *The Neolithic Cultures of the British Isles*, Cambridge 1954. Stuart Piggott: *Proc. Prehistoric Society*, NS, Vol. 2, No. 1, 143.
3. J. H. Craw, *Proceedings of the Society of Antiquaries of Scotland*, LVII, page 113.
4. D. Talbot Rice: *The Dark Ages*, London 1965, page 161. Carlo Carducci: *Antique Italian Gold and Silver*, London 1964, Plate 64a.
5. O. M. Dalton: *Antiquaries Journal*, 1922, page 89. Joan Liversidge: *Britain in the Roman Empire*, London 1968, Fig. 67. Cabrol: *Dictionnaire d'Archéologie Chrétienne*, vol. 2, Part 3. British Museum: The Mildenhall Treasure, 1947.
6. Baldwin Brown: *Burlington Magazine* XXIV, page 89.
7. A. C. O'Dell: The St Ninian's Isle Treasure, Edinburgh 1960.
8. Mgr. David McRoberts: The Ecclesiastical Significance of the St Ninian's Treasure, *Proceedings of the Society of Antiquaries of Scotland*, XCIV, 1960.
9. A. O. Curle: *Proceedings of the Society of Antiquaries of Scotland*, LXXXV, page 170. A. O. Curle: *The Treasure of Traprain Law*, Glasgow 1923. R. Laur-Belart: *Le Trésor d'Argent d'Epoque Romaine de Kaiseraugst*, Basle 1964.
10. G. E. P. and J. P. How: *English and Scottish Silver Spoons*, 3 vols., London, privately printed, 1952–57.
11. J. B. Ward Perkins: *Antiquaries' Journal*, XIX, page 313.
12. Carl R. af Ugglas: *Gottländska Silverskatter från Valdemarstågetstid*, Stockholm 1936. Ugglas and Granlund: *Skedasken av Biskopsform*, Stockholm 1943.

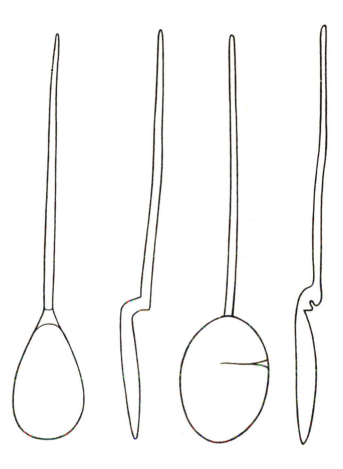

Fig. 34. Two late Roman spoons, front and side views. Silver, probably made in Britain. *Left:* from a villa at Foxcote, Suffolk—one of three. *Right:* with rudimentary junction feature. Probably fifth century. Cambridge University Museum of Archaeology.

Fig. 35. *Left* (two views) : brass spoon of rather crude construction, probably early Saxon. Cambridge University Museum of Archaeology. *Right:* Jutish ladle, pierced for use as a strainer, of the type normally associated with crystal balls mounted in strapwork, found in graves of high-ranking ladies. British Museum.

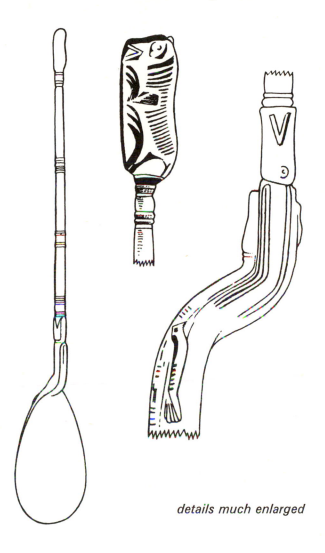

details much enlarged

Fig. 36. The Barham Down spoon, dug up at Barham Down in Kent. This shows clear affinities with late Roman spoons, but the decoration is unlike other Roman work.

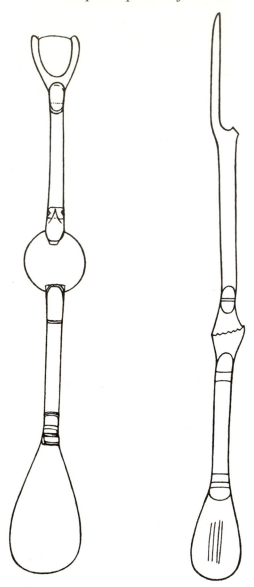

Fig. 37

Fig. 37. Two uncompleted sucket-forks from Sevington, Wiltshire. Part of a hoard of coins, ingots and scrap dated to c. 850; in the smaller version the fork tines had been drawn down and one broken off, clearly in the process of manufacture. The maker had broken it across and started work on a second, which had been roughed out from a casting and marked lightly with four animal's heads and an interlacing pattern, as well as being cross hatched over the web between the fork tines to indicate where metal was to be cut away—exactly as is still done in workshops of all kinds. The lines on the bowl of the right-hand specimen are from trial blows with a collet hammer. British Museum (see also Fig. 38).

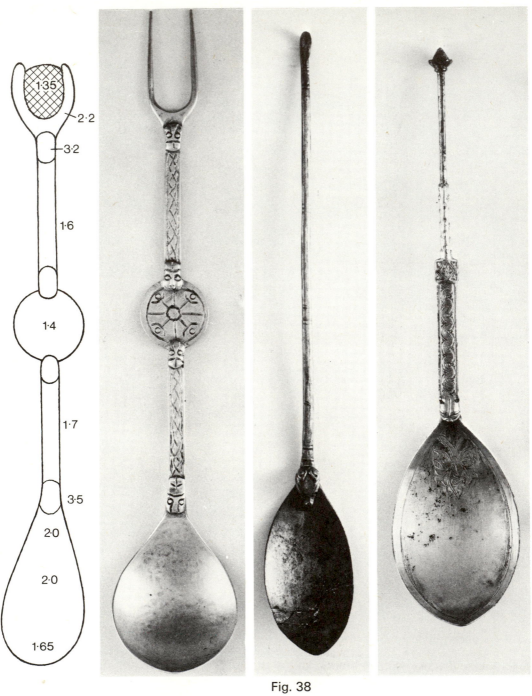

Fig. 38

Fig. 38. Pre-Conquest spoons

Left: the larger Sevington spoon, shown in outline as traced round the original and with thicknesses in millimetres added.

Second from left: the writer made an exact replica of the unfinished implement and finished it as it might have been intended to be—possibly a little small in the bowl, but otherwise without much margin for doubt. It is a rather ungainly piece of cutlery, but shows very clearly that forks were known in England before Alfred the Great came to the throne of Wessex.

Third from left: the St Ninian's spoon, with a very shallow bowl and a dog's head at the junction, formed as a separate piece and riveted on: it is the only one of its kind, and its origin is a matter for speculation, as the hoard contained at least one Roman piece (a one-pronged fork), as well as many which could be English, Scottish or Irish of the eighth century. National Museum of Antiquities of Scotland.

Right: one of four spoons from Iona. Originally claimed as French, these show no resemblance to any French spoons, and are more probably Anglo-Saxon. The suggestion that they could not be used for domestic purposes is also without foundation, an accurate replica having served the author on many occasions for eating porridge, and even fruit salad. The engraving shows no signs of ecclesiastical motifs, and the layout of the elements of the design resembles so conspicuously that of the Sevington spoon as to leave little doubt that it derives from Saxon rather than Norman predecessors. The fact that similar elements recur in sixteenth-century Scottish disc ends suggests a continuing tradition maintained probably through spoons of horn or wood which have not been preserved. National Museum of Antiquities of Scotland.

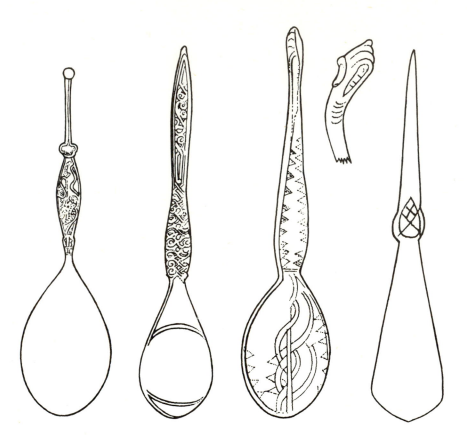

Fig. 39. Spoons of the Viking period. *Left:* silver, from Ribe, possibly English. Nationalmuseet, Copenhagen. *Left centre:* bone, from Bergen. Bergen Museum. *Right centre:* wood, from Oslo. Oslo Museum. *Right:* bone, from the Thames. London Museum.

Fig. 40. Two early Swedish spoons, showing the animal's head junction in realistic and conventionalised forms. *Left:* from Öland. *Right:* from Västergotland. Both probably fourteenth century. Stockholm, Statens Historiska Museum.

Fig. 41. *Left:* a fifth spoon, matching four dug up at Rouen. Rouen mark (a lamb and banner), c. 1300. Length 16·8 cm. Victoria and Albert Museum. *Centre:* a spoon of similar age, marked on the back of the stem MOP for Montpelier. *Right:* a fork of similar age, unmarked. Photographs by courtesy of Messrs Sotheby and Christie, Manson and Woods.

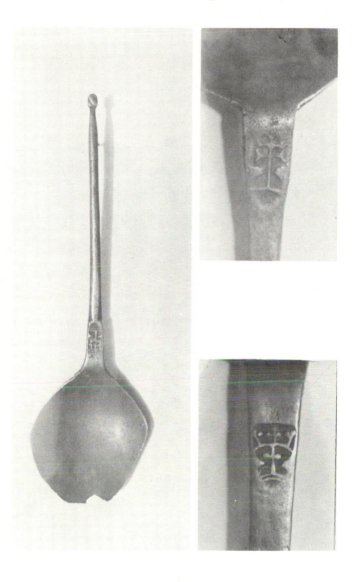

Fig. 42. Brass spoon with small wrythen finial and vestigial point to the bowl, the maker's mark simulating the animal's head of earlier silver spoons. The two marks, reproduced three times actual size, show how small changes produced a cross of Lorraine (top, as on the spoon) or a crowned leopard's head. The punches are clearly from the same workshop, probably Flanders c. 1400. Hague, Gemeentemuseum.

Fig. 43. Two early fourteenth-century spoons. *Left and centre:* silver acorn knop, mark an eagle displayed. Note the vestigial point to the bowl, and the suggestion of an animal's head at the junction. The bowl is level-edged and very shallow. Length 16·8 cm., weight 21 grams. *Right:* a similar spoon in brass, unmarked. Both probably Flemish.

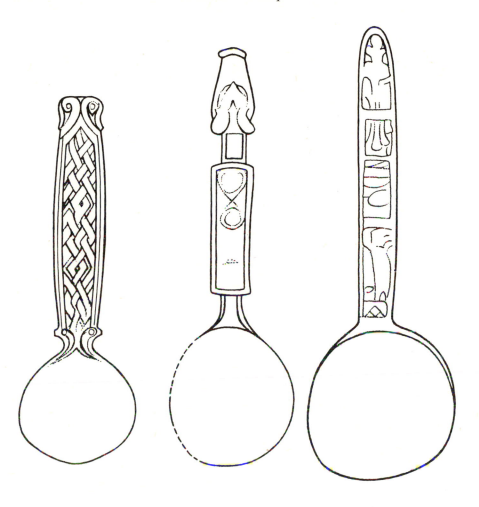

Fig. 44. Three horn spoons, all probably twelfth century. *Left:* from Sigtuna. Stockholm, Statens Historiska Museum. *Centre:* English, provenance unknown. Cambridge University Museum of Archaeology. *Right:* English, provenance unknown. British Museum.

Fig. 45. Brass spoons with degenerate animal's head junctions. *Left:* with a crowned hammer mark, closely resembling the animal's head in its main outlines. Length 15·8 cm. *Centre:* with an unidentified coat of arms. Both probably Flemish. *Right:* replica made by the author, marked with two punches, made to investigate the possibility of the mark being used as a thumb grip—which it certainly can be.

Fig. 46. Spoon in Dijon Museum, the details three times actual size, showing the vestigial animal's head. The spoon is awkward to hold, the stem being very thin and almost circular in cross section. Probably Burgundian, twelfth or thirteenth century—the only one of its kind known to the author.

5

National Developments

BEFORE going on to consider developments after about 1450, it might be as well to summarise the situation which obtained then, as far as present knowledge allows.

In Italy the ficulate form, having made a brief appearance, disappeared comparatively quickly, leaving the field divided between derivatives of the Pompeian hoof ends—the hoof increasingly stylised—and the flat-stemmed spoons of the north. In England and France the ficulate pattern was dominant in silver, although flat-stemmed spoons were probably still being made in brass. Over much of Europe horn and wooden spoons of a very simple type, occasionally tipped with silver, were in general use.

The next period to be considered is one of considerable national differentiation. Already perceptible by about 1450, this reaches its climax in the proliferation of local styles in seventeenth-century Holland and closes with the re-establishment of uniformity in spoons whose basic design has remained unchanged to the present day. Material and information from the period are very unevenly distributed, being extensive for England, seventeenth-century Holland and Scandinavia, and sketchy for France, Italy and Germany. This necessarily results in uneven treatment, and, from the point of view of this account, a further relevant factor is that in previous works the spoons of Britain have been dealt with exhaustively, those of Norway, Sweden and Denmark systematically, those of Holland unsystematically but fairly extensively, and the rest not at all. What follows is an attempt to fill in some of the gaps and to correlate previously published information. For this reason, it begins with English spoons, as being the best documented, followed by Scandinavian. In both cases the information presented is largely based on existing sources. The sections on the Netherlands and Italy contain information which is mostly previously unpublished but is regarded as reasonably well-established. Finally the sections on France, Germany and Poland are of necessity rather more sketchy and indicate the need for further detailed work. That such an account falls short of the ideal is frankly admitted, but the desirability of getting something recorded appeared to the writer to outweigh the disadvantage that the record is incomplete. In spite of some efforts it has been found impossible to extend research into countries now behind the Iron Curtain.

ENGLAND

With negligible exceptions, all English spoons made between 1400 and 1660 were of the ficulate pattern (Figs. 47–52), and variations affect principally the finials. Differences in stems and bowls also exist, and are important in diagnosing the age and provenance of unmarked specimens, or those whose marks have not been ascribed, but they are often subtle: they are dealt with in a most scholarly fashion by How.[1]

In the last quarter of the fifteenth century four integral and at least four separate finials were made, viz:

Integral
    Acorn knops
    Diamond points
    Seal tops
    Slip ends.
Separate
    Wrythen, ball and hexagon knops—also most seal tops
    Apostles and woodwoses and other full-length figures
    Maidenheads and other partial figures
    Lion sejants, owls and other livestock.

The sixteenth century was to see the disappearance of all the integral finials except the slip ends, and the rise of the separate seal top to a position of predominance: the succeeding century saw the supersession of the ficulate form by the trefid, whose descendants are the spoons of today.

English ficulate spoons were made in silver, in brass (in spite of enactments by the Pewterers' Company against this practice)[2] and in pewter: doubtless they were made in horn and wood as well, and a few are found in iron. It is interesting that the only material in which the pattern has survived to recent times is wood, in the form of cooking spoons.

Certain finials are found only in silver, and one (the horned head-dress) only in pewter, but the common ones were made in all metals, and the general form of these varies little from one material to another. Since the brass spoons were usually, if not always, tinned (the gilding of brass was illegal), confusion could easily arise between the metals, and the makers of base metal spoons took full advantage of this by striking marks of their own in the positions occupied by the hallmarks on silver ones—a practice which has extended into the age of electro-plate.

Although most English silver spoons were made, or at least marked in London, a proportion were made in the provinces. This proportion was very small in the sixteenth century, but rose rapidly in the first half of the seventeenth, with a particularly high concentration in the West of England and in East Anglia. In the former, the large quantity of Spanish silver acquired by West Country mariners was probably an important cause. In some cases these spoons bear the marks of authorised assay towns such as York, Norwich and Exeter, but many have obscure town marks sanctioned by no statute, and others have maker's marks only: a very few of these can be attributed with certainty to known silversmiths, but the majority can be assigned to an approximate date and area only by rather subtle distinctions of shape.

Workmanship of English ficulate spoons deteriorated somewhat during the sixteenth century, and catastrophically after the Restoration, but basic methods remained unchanged. Bowl and stem were generally forged in one piece, without the aid of a die for the tail, and finished by scraping and burnishing. Provincial spoons occasionally show clearly that they have been cast from London ones, the impressions of the London marks being distinguishable from the punched local marks. The finials were soldered on, with a front-to-back V joint in London and a halved joint in the provinces, and were normally gilt: it is unusual to find a spoon originally gilt all over, although some have been gilded at a later date, not infrequently to conceal repairs.

Fakes of English spoons are regrettably not uncommon, and this matter is discussed more fully elsewhere.

In the first quarter of the seventeenth century a form of spoon having an oval bowl and a flat, almost parallel stem, appears sporadically (Fig. 52). Although named the Puritan, it is much more likely that its inspiration was French. The type becomes slightly more plentiful in the Commonwealth period, and disappears soon after the Restoration.

A very rare kind of spoon produced at this time is a copy of an Italian hoof end and is the only variety made in England (before the days of art and craft schools) in which the stem and the bowl were separate pieces (Fig. 53).

The Restoration of Charles II in 1660 produced one of the most abrupt changes in the whole history of spoons. It introduced the trefid, with oval bowl, flat stem, enlarged and notched end and a beaded or ribbed rat tail below the bowl (Figs. 56 and 57). There is no question of evolution from the Puritans—the first trefids are hallmarked for 1660 and are of a pattern which was still being made in London forty years later, and contemporary ledgers record orders for 'French pattern spoons' by customers who brought their old ones in to be melted down.[3]

Although positive evidence is lacking, it seems probable that the trefid form derives from the Italian spoons, described as series B, in a previous chapter.

The trefid shape quickly spread to the provinces (Fig. 56), where some makers at first had trouble with the rat tail and continued to use a short triangular tail made over the edge of the anvil. By 1680 it was established everywhere (including Scotland), and variations with stems and the backs of bowls decorated by stamping or engraving (Fig. 57) (never by casting, as has sometimes been stated) began to appear in London. These were followed by plainer ones, in which the split trefid end was replaced by a wavy (dognose) outline and the stem became rounded in the middle (Fig. 59), and from these an easy transition led to the plain rat-tail spoons with ridged stems, rounded and upswept at the ends, which characterise the reigns of Queen Anne and George I, and which can be regarded as the first of the modern types (Fig. 59).

Some very puzzling brass spoons (Fig. 55), apparently made about 1680, are found in England and many parts of the Continent. They have round bowls, flat tapering stems terminating in either apostles or berries, and would not be considered as English were it not that many bear a mark of three or five spoons in a circle, surrounded by the description *DOUBLE WHITED*, which is also found on English-pattern apostle and seal tops. On every other ground these spoons would be classed as Continental; whether they were made in England by Continental immigrants or on the Continent for an

English customer is not known, but they differ so radically from any English forms that they cannot be accepted as part of the general sequence. A number of other brass spoons with peculiar finials may be associated with them.[4] The writer inclines to the view that they were made on the Continent for English troops engaged there, but does not pretend to have any evidence to support it. Only one English silver spoon of the form is known, a teaspoon marked for 1697 (Fig. 60).

Apart from these brass spoons, signs of continuing Continental influence are found in the evolution of the trefid into the wavy end—a process in which France led Britain by some twenty years. This is obviously connected with the stream of Huguenot refugees which continued for many years after the revocation of the Edict of Nantes in 1684, and contributed such famous names as Pierre Platel, Louis Cuny, Paul Lamerie and Augustine Courtauld. The dispersal of the Huguenots was a major cause of the uniformity of European styles in silver which is found in the early eighteenth century. Although a few small spoons, presumably made for children, are known from early Stuart times, it is not until well into the reign of Charles II that spoons of the same basic pattern begin to be made in different sizes, from very large serving spoons to small ones for stirring the new-fangled tea and coffee. Complete suites, covering the whole range of sizes, do not appear until the early eighteenth century.

The change to the trefid form marks an important stage in the evolution of social custom. Until the middle of the seventeenth century—and later in some places—it had been the custom for guests to bring their own eating implements when asked out to a meal, and they took care to have them easily recognisable, either by design or by personal engraving; the possibility of silver spoons being stolen by servants or other guests had to be borne in mind. Gradually, from the Restoration onwards, it became the practice to lay a complete set of cutlery on the table, all clearly marked with the owner's crest or initials. Individual sets were now made only for travelling, the components frequently either folding or unscrewing in the middle to pack inside a beaker. Complete canteens of this kind are very rare, but one reputedly used by Prince Charles Edward Stuart appeared some years ago in a London saleroom.

The appearance of different-sized spoons was accompanied by a proliferation of small silver articles such as apple corers, pastry markers, scissor cases and other domestic trifles, as well as by a short-lived revival of the combined spoon and fork—or sucket fork—known sporadically from the time of Alfred the Great.

Spoons with the stem formed as a scoop for marrow, as well as marrow spoons made double-ended to deal with large and small bones, occur very rarely before 1700, but are relatively common thereafter.

The introduction of a uniform style for an article in everyday use appears not infrequently to be accompanied by the production of a large number of more personal, but not always very useful, minor pieces. One might cite as examples the gold and jewelled swizzle sticks for cocktails offered around Christmas time by the more expensive shops, or the profusion of gadgets which convert a mass-produced car into a vehicle expressing the personality of its owner.

SCOTLAND

No indisputably Scottish spoons are known before about 1570, but for the next fifty years they are sufficiently numerous to be classifiable. There are four basic types:

1. *Seal tops*
These are quite unlike English seal tops, having broad, rather shallow, oval bowls and flat stems: the 'seals' resemble flattened thistles. Such spoons are exceedingly rare (Fig. 61).

2. *Disc ends*
These have similar oval bowls and flat stems, but terminate in circular discs, usually engraved with a rose pattern, and carry vestigial animal's heads (Fig. 62).

3. *Puritans*
Clumsy, heavy, and generally exceptionally badly made spoons having broad oval bowls and flat stems engraved on the front (Fig. 62).

4. *Slip ends*
Ficulate spoons with diamond-section stems, exactly copied from French originals (Fig. 61).

The first two classes have short rat tails, formed by hammering into a die, under the bowls. The third has no junction feature at all, and the fourth has the normal French ridged tail.

Hallmarks for Edinburgh make it quite certain that the earliest seal tops and disc ends were made before 1600, and the earliest slip ends not much later, while the Puritans all seem to date from after 1660. There is no mystery about the last two, but the others are difficult to explain.

The seal tops were certainly not copied from anything English: they might have been made by somebody who had heard about English seal tops but not seen one. Nothing of the kind could be suggested about the disc ends, which were being made many years before the introduction of the trefid to England. The earliest is dated by How[5] to about 1570. It seems unlikely that they were derived from a Scottish form, and far more probable that they are local versions of the Italian series B spoons referred to in a previous chapter. Mary Queen of Scots had an Italian secretary, Rizzio, and doubtless other Italians at her court.

It is noticeable that the earliest disc ends are small and have a simple outline, the parallel flat stem ending in a plain disc (Fig. 62): later ones are tapered throughout their length, and the stem is decorated with a clearly recognisable double animal's head design, basically similar to that found on the Sevington casting and the Iona spoons: this may be Scottish embellishment of a basically Italian design.

The Puritan spoons are in the same general tradition: the puzzle about them is that they are so heavy, clumsy and badly made that one cannot imagine anyone wanting to use them, or any reputable silversmith acknowledging having made them. A possible explanation is that they were a way of hoarding silver in times when proclamations commanding all citizens to give up their silver to finance the defence of the town were frequent.[6] Possibly spoons, being essential, were exempt from such ordinances. One can think of modern parallels.

The slip ends are obvious copies of French originals, quite understandable in a country whose ties with France were so strong: They are very rare.

After the Restoration, the trefid pattern did not take long to appear in Scotland, and by about 1680 plain trefids, hardly distinguishable from London ones, were being made as far north as Inverness. Thereafter evolution proceeded much as in England, although the decorated trefid is uncommon north of Newcastle, and Scottish wavy ends and rat tails are somewhat shorter and thicker set than their English counterparts.

Although sixteenth-century English spoons were not copied in Scotland, there is an interesting case of the reverse in the 'death's head' spoons made at York by Thomas Mangy in 1661; these have the same outline as Scottish disc ends, but are made like transitional trefids, with a short triangular tail under the bowl.

IRELAND

The system of hallmarking silver was not instituted in Dublin until 1638, which makes it difficult to know what sort of spoons were made before this date. Thereafter a few slip ends are known, including one with the second date letter, the B for 1639, and a seal top and an apostle have been recorded with marks which may be for Youghal.

Irish trefids are found from 1661, and development thereafter appears to have followed closely the fashions in England (Fig. 63).

It is quite possible that some of the unascribed marks on early types of spoon are Irish. Further research is needed on this subject.

Fig. 47. *Left:* acorn knop, unmarked, probably London, c·1400. *Centre:* early apostle spoon (St Thomas), London 1541, maker's mark a pheon? Length 16·5 cm. *Right:* diamond-point spoon, early leopard's head mark, probably London c. 1450. Photograph by courtesy of Messrs Christie, Manson and Woods.

Fig. 48. *Left:* a wrythen knop spoon with the rare mark of a leopard's head incorporating a letter in the tongue—possibly an early date letter—c. 1460. *Centre:* baluster knop, London 1554. *Right:* short seal top, London 1559. Photograph by courtesy of Messrs Christie, Manson and Woods.

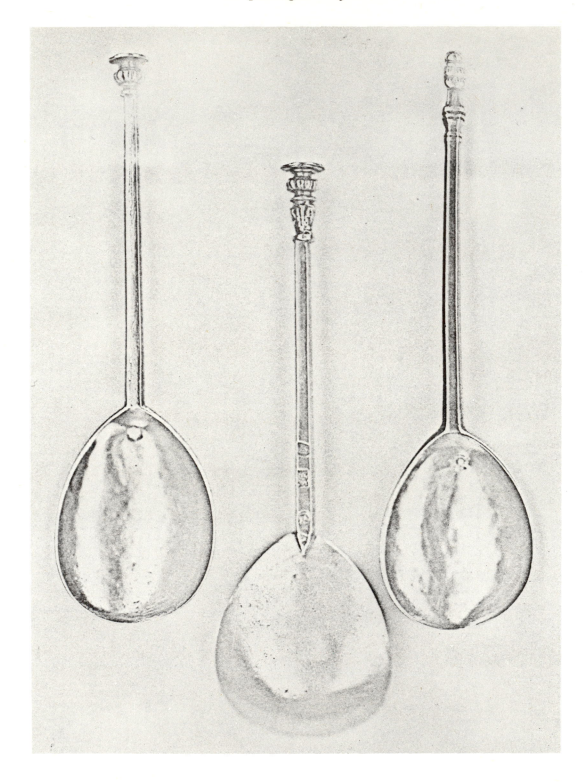

Fig. 49. *Left:* short seal top, London 1592, maker's mark C enclosing a star. Length 15·7 cm., weight 35 grams. *Centre:* baluster seal top, London 1637, maker's mark H. Length 16·5 cm., weight 45 grams. *Right:* lion sejant, maker's mark in bowl only, a flowerhead; West Country, possibly Launceston. Length 16·2 cm., weight 35 grams. A picture taken by laying the spoons on the bed of a Xerox copier and operating in the normal way; included to show this method as a means of producing a record quickly.

Fig. 50

Fig. 51

Figs. 50–51 (front and back views of same three spoons). English apostle spoons, showing minor variations. *Left:* St John, with engraved nimbus at 45° to the axis, marked high in the bowl with a device in a pelleted circle, halved joint to the finial. Early sixteenth century. Length 16·6 cm., weight 42 grams. *Centre:* St Paul, London 1603, maker's mark C enclosing W—one of many marks featuring a crescent or C enclosing another symbol, probably representing a firm rather than an individual. There is no evidence for the claim that this is the mark of Christopher Waiste. Length 18·2 cm., weight 62 grams. *Right:* St Paul, a different figure, maker's mark in the bowl and thrice on the stem—a berry (?); probably West of England c. 1670. Length 16·8 cm., weight 33 grams. This spoon has been repaired right across the bowl. The back of the St John shows that ancient initials $\frac{R}{RC}$ have been filled with silver solder and initials $\frac{IC}{M}$ cut over them; the solder has fretted down by solution to show the original set, a process which takes a long time.

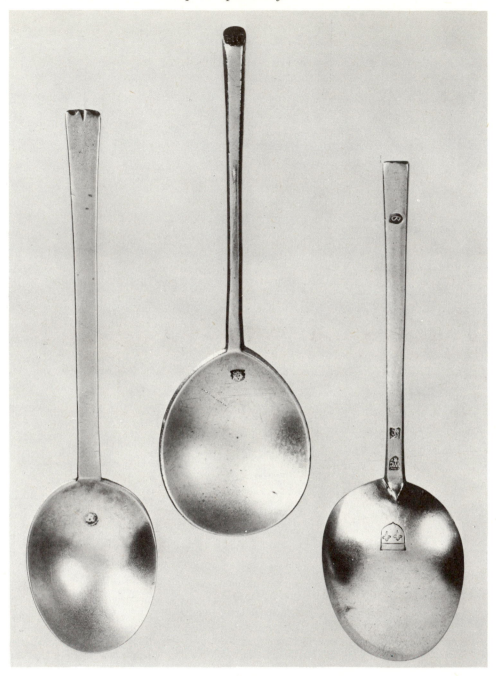

Fig. 52. *Left:* notched top Puritan spoon, pricked with the date 1671, mark BR, probably Bristol. *Centre:* slip end spoon, London 1639, maker's mark probably TH. Length 16·8 cm., weight 42 grams. *Right:* Puritan spoon, London 1639, maker's mark WC. The average Puritan is 16–18 cm. in length and weighs 45–50 grams. Photograph by courtesy of Messrs Christie, Manson and Woods.

Fig. 53. Three of the rare English hoof-ended spoons. *Left:* London 1622, maker's mark D enclosing C. *Centre:* London 1652, maker's mark AF. *Right:* London 1612, maker's mark a crescent enclosing W. Photograph by courtesy of Messrs Christie, Manson and Woods.

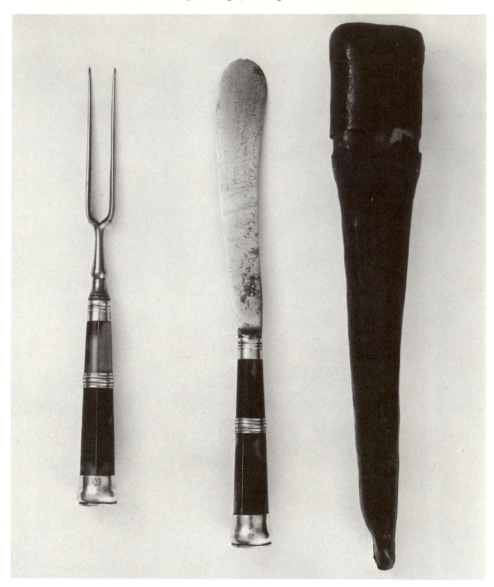

Fig. 54. Knife and fork with steel blade and tines, mounted in tortoiseshell handles piqué in silver, contained in a leather case. Mark on blade and mounts AB. Possibly Scottish, late seventeenth century. Length of knife, 17·1 cm.

Fig. 55. Three base metal spoons. *Left:* seal top, latten (a kind of brass), maker's mark IW, probably London, early seventeenth century. *Centre:* an acorn knop, pewter, unmarked, c. 1500. *Right:* an apostle, with grooved stem and Continental pattern bowl, marked in the bowl with three spoons between RW; originally tinned all over, thus resembling silver. Origin not clearly established. Length 17·5 cm.

Fig. 56. *Left:* trefid, Edinburgh 1694, maker James Penman, assay master John Borthwick. Length 19·8 cm., weight 55 grams. *Right:* trefid, Exeter 1702, maker John Elston. Length 19·2 cm., weight 38 grams. The uniformity of style achieved by 1700 is well shown.

Fig. 57. Three trefids. *Left:* with decorated (lace) back, marked with a rose and RS (cf. Jackson: *English Goldsmiths and Their Marks,* page 483, line 5), possibly Carlisle c. 1680. *Centre:* London 1689, maker's mark WS for William Scarlett. *Right:* a transitional type, with short rat tail, mark a tower, possibly Newcastle, c. 1688; similar spoons are known from Norwich and the West Country somewhat earlier. An average London trefid is 18–20 cm. long and weighs 45–55 grams. Photograph by courtesy of Messrs Christie, Manson and Woods.

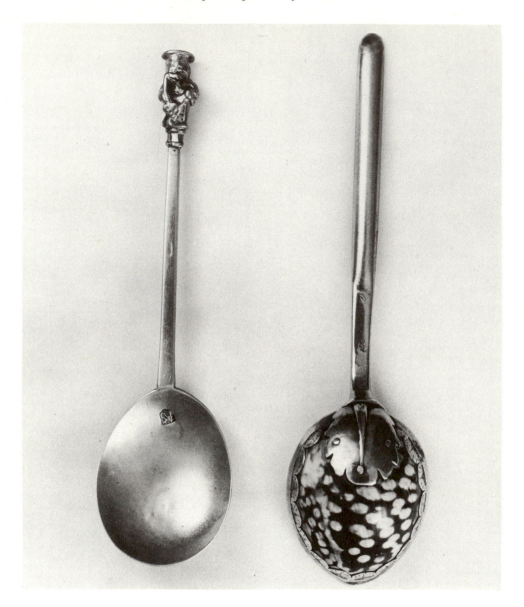

Fig. 58. *Left:* a very crudely cast St Peter; mark AS, once in the bowl and thrice on the stem. Almost certainly West of England. Length 17·8 cm. *Right:* a cowrie shell bowled spoon with marrow scoop stem. Maker's mark only: WC (a London maker c. 1675: cf. Jackson: *English Goldsmiths and Their Marks*, page 136, line 20). Such composite spoons are very rare from London, but are more common on the Continent.

Fig. 59. *Left:* a wavy (dognose) end spoon, a form made in Paris by 1680, but not in London before 1700; London 1703. Length 20·2 cm., weight 54 grams. *Centre:* a marrow scoop, London 1716. *Right:* spoon and two-pronged fork by Andrew Archer, London 1714. Length of spoon 19 cm., weight 54 grams.

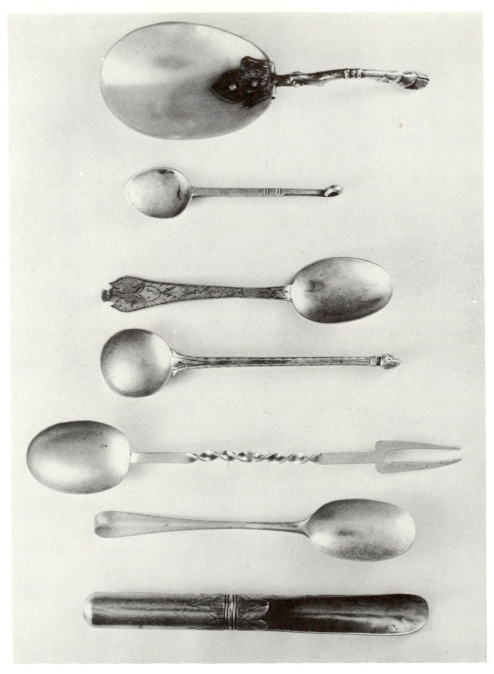

Fig. 60

Fig. 60. Seven small spoons. From top to bottom: 1) a mother-of-pearl spoon with silver hoof stem, c. 1630; 2) a snuff spoon, unmarked, from a Charles II snuffbox; 3) an engraved trefid teaspoon, maker's mark only PLB, c. 1680, length 10·2 cm.; 4) a teaspoon of Danish pattern, fully marked, London 1697; 5) a sucket fork, unmarked, c. 1680; 6) a rat tail teaspoon, London c. 1715; 7) an apple corer or cheese scoop, maker's mark only IH, c. 1690.

The last few years of the seventeenth century saw a proliferation of small domestic pieces of silver in a wide variety of patterns. The majority have either no marks or a maker's mark only, and could easily be overlooked.

Number 4 is one of the very few recognisable copies of a Scandinavian piece known to have been made in London; the placing of the marks (three close together near the bowl and the fourth near the finial) supports the claim that it is in original condition, although such a piece would normally be suspect.

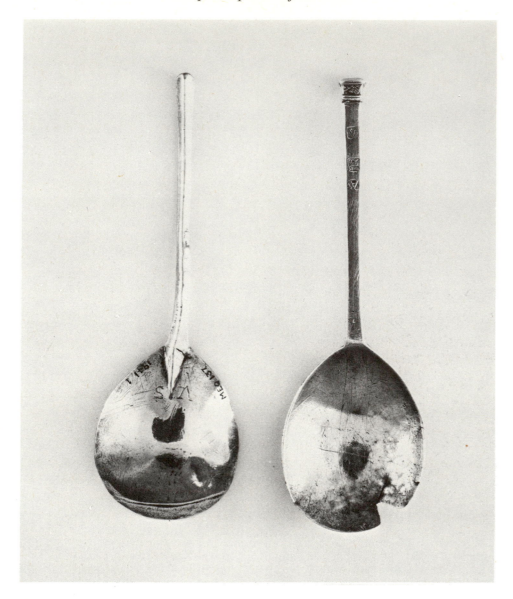

Fig. 61. Early Scottish spoons based on Continental, probably French, originals. *Left:* slip end of conventional French pattern, marked for Edinburgh, c. 1600. *Right:* seal top, the bowl and stem of Continental rather than English form, marked on the front of the stem for Edinburgh; maker's mark William Cok, c. 1573. National Museum of Antiquities of Scotland.

Fig. 62. Three more early Scottish spoons, all in the National Museum of Antiquities of Scotland. *Left:* disc end, of simple early outline, engraved 1589, marked for Canongate, maker's mark GC (cf. Jackson: *English Goldsmiths and Their Marks*, page 514, lines 1 and 2, both taken from this spoon). *Centre:* disc end, one of a set made for the Cunningham family, Edinburgh, probably 1585: the rat tail is characteristic of these spoons, but actually contributes nothing to strength. *Right:* a Puritan, Edinburgh, 1665–7, by David Bog. This has no rat tail, and is badly made and roughly engraved. Length 18·2 cm.

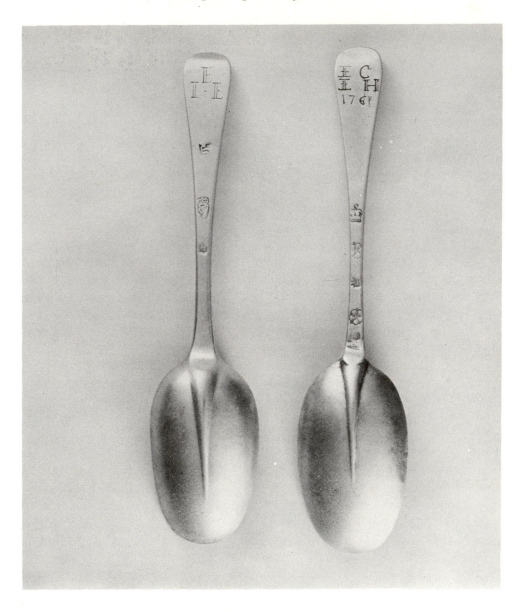

Fig. 63. *Left:* an Irish rat tail spoon, Dublin 1706, maker Edward Barrett. Length 17.3 cm., weight 49 grams. *Right:* a late Norwich spoon, mark AH with a separate rose and crown in the manner of the Heaselwood family (cf. Jackson: *English Goldsmiths and Their Marks*, page 318). Arthur Heaselwood II died in 1665; his widow, Elizabeth, made and marked silver EH until c. 1700. This spoon was probably made by their son, also Arthur, who is recorded as free in 1702, after the Norwich office had apparently ceased operations. Length 18·8 cm., weight 43 grams.

SCANDINAVIA

Scandinavian silver spoons which can confidently be dated before about 1600 conform closely to a single type: they have rather large round bowls, short stems and conspicuous knops. It was not until the seventeenth century that stems began to extend to lengths comparable with those of English spoons; thereafter proliferation of new varieties was rapid, and clear regional characteristics can be traced.

A group of spoons in the Statens Historiska Museum, Stockholm, described by Ugglas,[7] has already been referred to. These are shortened versions of the Rouen animal's head spoons, and are probably of similar date. A selection of spoons of very similar outline, but with rather large icosahedral knops (Fig. 64), in the National Museet, Copenhagen,[8] is probably a little later, but clearly of the same family: it is significant that in many of these the previously well-modelled animal's head has degenerated to a double moulding below which the stem thins perceptibly before running into the bowl, which it joins without any tail or other strengthening feature.

Although finials are normally large, a few small Danish diamond points occur, and these are comparable with the Brechin and Montrose spoons from Scotland, the obvious difference being that the Danish spoons have larger bowls and thicker stems.

By the middle of the sixteenth century a new finial in the form of a hollow crown (often hung with rings) was being produced in Sweden, and the stem was not infrequently twisted (Figs. 66 and 67).

Spoons of this form were made in Sweden well after the middle of the eighteenth century and inscriptions leave no doubt that they were christening presents. They are well adapted for conveying liquids from bowls, but extremely awkward to use with anything sticky or solid.

In the first quarter of the seventeenth century a recognisable variant of this form, with a short twisted stem and plain ball knop, was being made in Bergen: the animal's head is represented by a short flat portion, chased with two or more lines, linking the bowl to the stem. Several such spoons with marks assignable to known Bergen makers are illustrated by Krohn-Hansen.[9] At the same time, the crown finial type was being made in Skien,[10] not far from Oslo.

A very simple ball-knopped spoon from Nyborg is of interest because it is intermediate in form between the Danish and Dutch versions of the same article (Fig. 65): the complete absence of any tail behind the bowl in Danish spoons distinguishes the two.

Development during the seventeenth century proceeded along four main lines:

1. The short flat linking the twisted stem to the bowl in the early Bergen spoons was extended to be as long as the twisted part, and was decorated with engraving. Spoons of this form with plain ball knops are Norwegian (Figs. 66 and 67), but similar spoons with apostle finials were made in the Dutch province of Friesland and in Hoorn between 1615 and 1690, and obviously related types in Emden and the province of Groningen, as well as in the Rhineland. These are fully dealt with in the sections on Germany and the Netherlands.

2. Spoons with plain, almost circular, stems grooved down the front, and flattened triangular knops ornamented as berries or with cherub's heads on both sides became

predominant in Denmark and common in Norway (Figs. 68 and 69). The groove in the front of the stem appears to simulate that found in most horn spoons, and suggests a derivation from horn originals, as has been mentioned earlier.

3. An entirely new form appeared, in which the lower part of the stem was round and the upper part was flattened, engraved, and frequently finished with an oblique indented outline (Figs. 66 and 72). An example from Skien of this type is dated 1614, but the majority are somewhat later. This kind of spoon bears no very obvious resemblance to anything found elsewhere.

4. Towards the end of the century, spoons with relatively thin flat stems appear. A characteristic Danish form has a separate terminal formed as a rose, cast and soldered on (Figs. 70 and 71), but in later versions the stem is thin, widening towards a rounded end, and engraved all over. This design became general after about 1700, and persisted well into the eighteenth century. Although not unlike the English trefids in outline, it appears to owe nothing to them: Danish trefids, which are rare, are closely similar to English ones, but do not appear to have been made before 1700.

A number of Scandinavian spoons do not fit into this fourfold classification. Four, in the National Museet, Copenhagen, closely dateable to about 1620, have bowls and stems of forms very similar to those of some Dutch spoons of Group A, and apostle finials from the same patterns as those made in Friesland during the seventeenth century, but no tails behind the bowls. They were the work of Johann Neue, who went to Copenhagen in 1621 and worked there until 1628.

In some cases at least, Scandinavian spoons were cast to size and shape and finished by scraping. An example illustrated (Fig. 68) would almost pass as Graeco-Roman, were it not for the double cherub's head finial and maker's marks. The practice was not, however, confined to the short spoons, two in the National Museet with flat, almost parallel stems from Køge exhibiting clear casting flaws.

When the Scandinavian makers went over to making spoons from sheet, they tended to use it rather thin. The results, devoid of any reinforcement where the bowl joins the stem, are on the flimsy side. The use of a strengthening rat tail or drop, as in English spoons, was uncommon, although not unknown. Quite frequently it was suggested by engraving, a process which added nothing to the strength and in fact slightly reduced it.

The majority of early Scandinavian spoons, where marked at all, have maker's marks only, placed on the back of the stem close to the bowl, although some of those with flattened stems are marked near the terminal: this practice seems to have been particularly common in Bergen. Danish spoons not infrequently have the maker's mark struck twice, as does much other Danish silver.

After the middle of the eighteenth century, Scandinavian spoons in general conformed to other European styles, but early types were made in Norway and Sweden, particularly in country districts, until quite recently. Although beyond the range of the present survey, it is of interest to note that a variety of the 'Old English' pattern, common to all Scandinavian countries about 1800, and also made in North Germany, Poland and Holland, is found in Scotland and Ireland, but never in England. These spoons, having pointed terminals and rather pointed egg-shaped bowls, are so similar in appearance that it is possible to lay a table with examples from six different countries without anyone noticing the difference. Spoons of Scandinavian origin are not infrequently offered for sale in Scotland as being Scottish provincial, the result of a perfectly understandable mistake which only a detailed knowledge of marks can remedy, while spoons by some Scottish makers, especially James Comfute of Perth, are markedly East Baltic in style.

GERMANY, POLAND AND AUSTRIA

The idea of Germany as a single entity is so recent as to make it unsuitable as a general designation for a historical study, and the complexity of its organisation from the middle ages to the nineteenth century makes it a major field of investigation in itself—an undertaking not facilitated by the existence of the Iron Curtain. A few ideas, relating to points of contact with other countries, will be sketched here.

Seven different kinds of spoon can with reasonable confidence be attributed to present or former parts of Germany:

1. Spoons with long flat stems tapering to the finial, and round bowls devoid of any junction feature. These are found right across Northern Europe from Danzig to the Normandy coast, often with crown finials but occasionally with figures; from their distribution, they might be described as the 'Hanseatic' type. In general, those from the East are longer, wider, and have a deeper drop from stem to bowl than those from the West, some of which are not far different from English spoons in outline, although distinguished by their rectangular stems, absence of junction reinforcement and position of marks (Figs. 74, 75, 83 and 84).

2. Spoons having almost parallel stems, joined to the bowl by a short flat decorated section. There is considerable variation within the group, from very massive spoons with hexagonal stems and elaborate cast ornament from Breslau (Fig. 77), to delicate ones with twisted stems and lion sejant finials from the Rhineland (Fig. 78). Both show a rather tenuous connection with the short-stemmed early spoons from Bergen, but would never be confused with them. The stems of the massive variety are very frequently engraved all along their length with Latin inscriptions.

3. Short brass spoons, with fig-shaped bowls, lozenge-section stem and figure knops, cast in one piece. These could well be early, before 1600 (Fig. 105).

4. Spoons with bowls of maplewood (sometimes rock-crystal: the shapes are identical) tipped with tapering polygonal silver sleeves usually carrying apostles (Fig. 94). The fact that some of the apostles are from the same patterns as those used in Groningen and Friesland in the seventeenth century gives some clue as to the probable region of origin. At least three series of these apostle figures exist, and they are found as far south as Switzerland: the Dutch series, when used on Dutch spoons, have invariably been cast from patterns from which the nimbi have been filed away, but both complete and mutilated figures are found on wooden spoons which appear to be German. A variant having a ball-knop, associated sometimes with a twisted stem, may be earlier, but most

of these spoons seem to date between 1600 and 1640. It seems probable that they derive from all-wooden prototypes.

5. Spoons with maplewood bowls and hollow silver stems ending in flat terminals, the stem being continued under the bowl to form a flat rib on which the spoon will stand. Because of this feature, these are generally described as medicine spoons, although why one should wish to pour out medicine and leave it standing in the spoon is not clear. They were also made in silver throughout, especially in southern Germany.[11]

6. Spoons with oval bowls and hollow twisted stems, occasionally decorated with filigree. This seems to be a south German variety, emanating largely from Nuremburg and Augsburg (Fig. 80), possibly inspired by Italian originals, and almost certainly based on spoons made of wood.

7. Recognisable trefids and wavy ends (Fig. 81), often made to fold in the middle and generally engraved. Occasionally bowl and stem are separate pieces, but perfectly normal trefids are also found; they are generally lighter than English or Dutch ones. A type apparently peculiar to Salzburg is made of horn, decorated with pressed ornament and mounted with silver.

In addition to these seven groups, spoons of distinctive form were made at Emden about 1620 (Fig. 107). These are so closely linked to the Friesland and Groningen spoons that they are treated with them, in the section on the Netherlands, as are the spoons of Enkhuizen type (Figs. 115 and 116), examples of which are found with marks which are probably German.

The importation of the Italian hoof end pattern into Holland extended into Germany: a point of difference is that the hoof end is generally turned down on German spoons, always up on Dutch ones (Fig. 80).

Not surprisingly, a large number of rather fancy spoons made of agate, coral, cowrie shell and other exotic materials were made in Germany. Such feature largely in museum exhibits, but appear to have little relevance to the development of spoons as a whole. They appear to be early examples of those articles, well known in shops today, which make impressive presents but are almost totally useless.

FRANCE

That the spoons of France should be treated in much less detail than those of the Netherlands may seem odd, but there are good reasons why it should be so. Not only is the very size of the country discouraging, but what is perhaps more important, previous literature is very scanty and museum organisation is, to put it mildly, variable. Added to this is the devastation produced by the Revolution, which resulted in pre-revolutionary silver of French origin becoming exceedingly scarce.

The earliest surviving French silver spoons of the period now being considered show conspicuous resemblances to those made contemporaneously in England, with enough points of difference to render them interesting. They are all of ficulate form, mostly slip ends, although some ball and cone knops occur. The stems are lozenge-shaped and usually are continued under the bowls as well-formed tails, showing evidence of the use of a die. Marks, which are unfortunately not fully documented, are struck on one facet of the back of the stem, near the tip in slip ends and near the bowl in other types, and frequently consist of a letter surmounted by a crowned fleur-de-lys. The earliest example for which a firm date has been claimed is a ball knop from Rouen, supposedly about 1410.[12] Possibly a few years later is a spoon whose knop resembles a pineapple, which has a much shorter tail under the bowl and a mark which may be for Orleans (Fig. 87). Faith Dennis[13] illustrates a set of six rather similar spoons, ascribed to a Troyes maker (Rouaine) of about 1645; this date seems improbable, but perhaps the goldsmiths of Troyes were conservative.

Slip ends are rather more common. They are all very similar, and the majority show signs of having been buried, to such an extent that the marks are indecipherable (Fig. 87). They are somewhat lighter than the earliest English slip ends, which date from about 1500.[14]

Baluster finials are the third ficulate type represented. They are generally rather small, and are dated conjecturally to about 1500. The baluster finial does not seem to appear in England before 1550, but when it does it looks much more developed than in the French spoons.

There are a few figure finials on bronze spoons in French museums but their origin is uncertain: and no example of a French silver apostle, lion sejant or seal top has come to light. It seems improbable that all such could have escaped detection and one is forced to the conclusion that they were never made. The fact that they are also absent in Italy, but common east of the Rhine, suggests that English makers drew their inspiration for general design and for finials from separate sources. The same trend towards ovality in the shape of the bowl as appears in English spoons is shown by an example from Rouen, dated to the second half of the sixteenth century (Fig. 87).

Two outstanding spoons in the British Museum illustrate something of the splendour of French goldsmith's work that has perished. One, of silver enamelled and a simple ficulate in form, could be fifteenth century (Fig. 88). The other, a berry finial spoon with demountable stem, has a well-modelled animal's head grasping the bowl in its mouth: the screwed stem joints may indicate a somewhat later date. Both are considered to be Burgundian, but nothing is known of their history: they are illustrated and discussed by How.

The next type of spoon to be made in France was quite different. The bowl was oval, the stem flat and nearly parallel-sided, cut off squarely at the end and finished with two shallow notches (Fig. 89). The conspicuous tail under the bowl remains, and is sometimes extended a short distance up the stem, providing a strengthening feature whose merits have been recognized by modern makers of plastic spoons.

This form, closely resembling the English puritan (which was presumably copied from it) appears to have persisted until about 1640: at what stage it was replaced by the trefid is not established, but it must have been well before 1660, in which year fully-developed trefids were introduced into England from France. Thereafter the shape of the terminal evolved rapidly towards smooth lobing, as illustrated by a Paris spoon of before 1681 which has a wavy end (Fig. 89). A possible intermediate stage is shown by the Clermont-Ferrand fork of about 1670 (Fig. 89). A wavy-ended spoon decorated with black enamel, now in the Fitzwilliam Museum, is almost certainly French and of this period.

Further development took the form of elaboration of the wavy-ended and succeeding round-ended varieties. French goldsmiths led Europe in the use of dies for stamping decoration on to spoon stems, and most of the decorated patterns found in other countries can be matched some years earlier in Paris.

Besides the silver spoons, a great variety of brass and pewter ones occur. The tapered flat-stemmed form referred to earlier may well have been made after the fourteenth century, but slip ends, baluster and figure-finial spoons of ficulate type were produced also, together with some hoof ends of Italianate appearance. In pewter, spoons of Jan Steen and trefid shapes were certainly made, both spoons and moulds having survived.

The writer found an interesting group of brass spoons in a shop in Rouen: they have egg-shaped bowls and almost circular disc ends, stamped with maker's marks (Fig. 90). Whether they are derived from trefids or directly from Italian disc ends remains a matter for conjecture. Bearing in mind the lead which France maintained in design, these spoons may be rather earlier than they seem.

It is very likely that a large number of early French spoons exist in private collections as well as in museums: possibly the account given here will bring some of them out of hiding, and enable a fuller study to be made.

SWITZERLAND

Most early Swiss spoons were of wood, sometimes tipped with silver, and they are not easy to distinguish from German ones. Examples in silver are rare, but from the beginning of the seventeenth century a distinctive form appears certainly in Berne and Zurich, and possibly elsewhere. This has a rather small fig-shaped bowl soldered to a gracefully curved hollow stem, surmounted by a cast terminal—usually an apostle (Fig. 91). The distinct swelling of the stem below the bowl suggests affinities with the German 'medicine spoons' but, unlike them, the Swiss spoons will not stand or even rest straight on the table.

Where these spoons have apostle finials, they are unmistakeably derived from the same set of patterns as those used in Holland and the Rhineland.

The peculiar shape of the stem indicates that these spoons were used for eating from bowls rather than from plates.

In addition to this distinctively Swiss form, spoons of south German type were made in Switzerland, including the variety having a twisted hollow stem (Fig. 92). In country districts, spoons made from horn were generally used. Many have long inscriptions engraved on the back of the bowl (Fig. 92).

By about 1680 trefids of normal type were being made in Switzerland: one, from Zug, is in the museum in Zurich.

NOTES

1. How: *English and Scottish Silver Spoons*, London 1952–57.
2. F. G. Hilton Price: *Old Base Metal Spoons*, London 1908.
3. Ibid. Price quotes from the ledgers of Blanchard and Childe.
4. Christopher A. Pearl, *Connoisseur*, April and July 1970, shows several examples of brass apostles.
5. How, op. cit., vol. 2.
6. There are many such, particularly from the seventeenth century.
7. Ugglas: *Skedasken av Biskopsform*, Stockholm 1943, Figs. 1, 2 & 3.
8. G. B. Boesen and C. A. Bøje: *Old Danish Silver*, translated by R. Kay, Copenhagen 1949.
9. T. Krohn-Hansen: *Bergens Gullsmedkunst fra Langstiden*, Bergen 1957.
10. Inger Marie Kwall Lie: *Renessance Sølv fra Skien*, Kunstindustriemuseet i Oslo, 1965.
11. H. Brunner: *Old Table Silver*, London 1967, Fig. 221.
12. How, op. cit., vol. 3, Plate 8.
13. Faith Dennis: *Three Centuries of French Domestic Silver*, New York, Metropolitan Museum of Art, 1960.
14. How, op. cit., vol. 3, Plate 18.

Fig. 64. Two small spoons, Danish (or possibly North German), fifteenth or early sixteenth century. Copenhagen, Nationalmuseet.

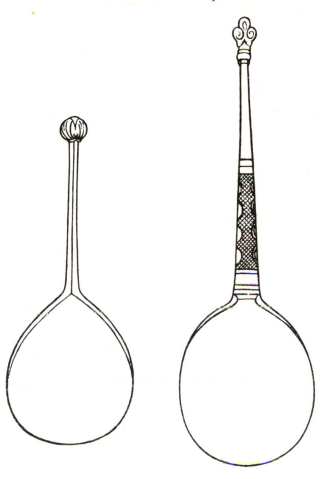

Fig. 65. *Left:* simple ball-knop silver spoon, dug up at Nyborg, unmarked, c. 1560. Nyborg Museum. *Right:* silver spoon with tapered flat stem of 'Hanseatic' type. Maker's mark CS for Christian Nielsen Stub of Køge, c. 1670. Køge Museum.

Fig. 66

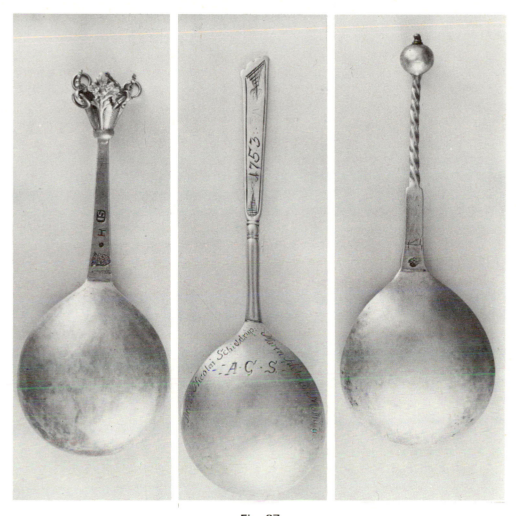

Fig. 67

Figs. 66–67 (front and back views of same three Scandinavian spoons). *Left:* a late version of an early pattern of Swedish spoon, known from c. 1600. Söderkoping 1765, maker Johan Söderdahl. Such pieces were made as christening spoons long after the style had fallen into disuse. Length 14 cm., weight 32 grams. *Centre:* a flat-stemmed Norwegian spoon, maker's mark JP for Jorgen Petterson of Bergen, 1666–1683, later engraved 1753 (cf. Krohn-Hansen: *Bergens Gullsmedkunst,* Plate 24). Length 16 cm., weight 27 grams. *Right:* Norwegian ball-knopped spoon, maker's mark AB, c. 1630. The earliest versions have only a very short flat portion between the bowl and the stem; this pattern closely resembles contemporary Dutch spoons of Group C (see text), but the latter never have plain ball knops, while Norwegian spoons apparently never carry apostles.

Fig. 68

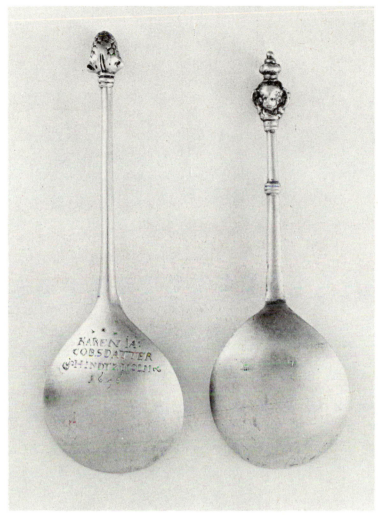

Fig. 69

Figs. 68–69 (front and back views of same two spoons). *Left:* spoon with grooved stem and berry finial. Engraved KAREN IACOBSDATTER. HINDIZHOLM. 1656. Norwegian, but also found in Denmark and Sweden, very popular 1640–70. Length 15·4 cm., weight 39 grams. *Right:* cast cherub's head spoon, one piece, finished by scraping. Marks unidentified, probably East Baltic, c. 1600. Length 14·6 cm., weight 41 grams.

Fig. 70

Fig. 71

Figs. 70–71 (front and back views of same spoons). Three Scandinavian flat-stemmed spoons. *Left:* Swedish trefid, maker's mark BB, probably Bangst Bongstrom, c. 1697. Length 17 cm., weight 41 grams. *Centre:* Danish rose end, the rose soldered with a scarfed joint, unmarked, c. 1658, probably Copenhagen area. Length 17·5 cm., weight 37 grams. *Right:* Norwegian, maker's mark LQ for Lars Larsen Quist of Bergen, c. 1705. Length 17·4 cm., weight 33 grams.

Fig. 72. *Left:* Norwegian spoon of very base silver, engraved 1731, unmarked. Length
17·2 cm. *Centre:* folding double-ended spoon, maker's mark FS for Ferdinand Seht of
Stockholm, 1688–1731. Length 18 cm., weight 45 grams. *Right:* spoon with cast stem
decoration, probably East Baltic, mid seventeenth century, unmarked. Length 15·8 cm.,
weight 42 grams.

Fig. 73. Two unusual spoons, both probably Scandinavian. *Left:* hung with rings, probably Norwegian, early eighteenth century. Length 14·2 cm., weight 40 grams. *Right:* spoon with stem wreathed with vine leaves, and with dove finial, the back of the bowl engraved in the style of c. 1680 with acanthus leaves. Spoons of similar pattern are mentioned in the inventory of Henry VIII's plate, but this is clearly later. Length 15·6 cm., weight 42 grams.

Fig. 74

Fig. 75

Figs. 74–75 (front and back views of same spoons). Apostle spoons contrasted. *Left:* St Peter on a spoon of obviously Continental origin, maker's mark only, probably AV, unidentified; engraved with initials and a typical Hanseatic League type of merchant's mark. Silver below sterling standard, originally gilt all over. Long halved joint to finial. Engraved very roughly with a cross in the position occupied by the animal's head on early spoons. The apostle is of English type, but not of any known series. Length 18·4 cm., weight 48 grams. *Right:* the Master, London 1619, maker's mark WR. A typical spoon of the period, although Master spoons are less common than those with figures of the twelve. Length 18 cm., weight 53 grams. The differences between the two are most apparent in the stems, and in the absence of any junction feature on the St Peter. The figures are stylistically very similar, proportioned as dolls rather than as real people, contrasting in this respect with the series used on the Dutch apostle spoons. The St Peter is tentatively ascribed to the Hamburg area, c. 1580.

Fig. 76

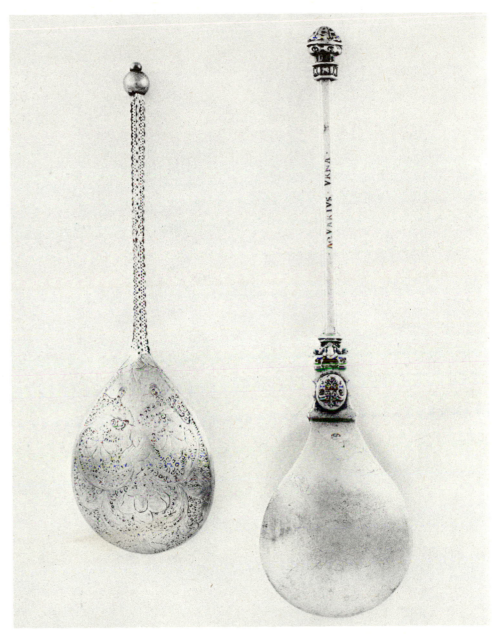

Fig. 77

Figs. 76–77 (front and back views of same spoons). *Left:* ball-knopped spoon of ficulate form, engraved all over. Unmarked, probably Polish or Russian, sixteenth or early seventeenth century. Length 17·3 cm., weight 43 grams. *Right:* massive ball-knopped spoon of a pattern particularly associated with Breslau; marks difficult to read, c. 1580. The stem is engraved PORTAT ACQUAM MADIDA FLUVIALIS. ACQUARIUS URNA: such inscriptions are common on these spoons. Length 21·6 cm., weight 81 grams.

Fig. 78. Two spoons from the Rhineland. *Left:* lion sejant affronté, Cologne, before 1650 (cf. Rosenberg, no. 2696). Maker's mark an animal's head. Length 17·4 cm., weight 31 grams. *Right:* lion sejant, probably Düsseldorf (a demi-lion above an anchor, maker's mark a housemark in conforming shield). Length 16·9 cm., weight 31 grams. The inversion of the plain and twisted portions of the stem distinguishes these spoons from those made in Holland at the same period.

Fig. 79. Silver combined spoon and fork. Flemish, Tournai c. 1630. Although not German, this spoon is included here because of its markedly Teutonic styling. Combined implements of this kind are known from German sources. British Museum photograph.

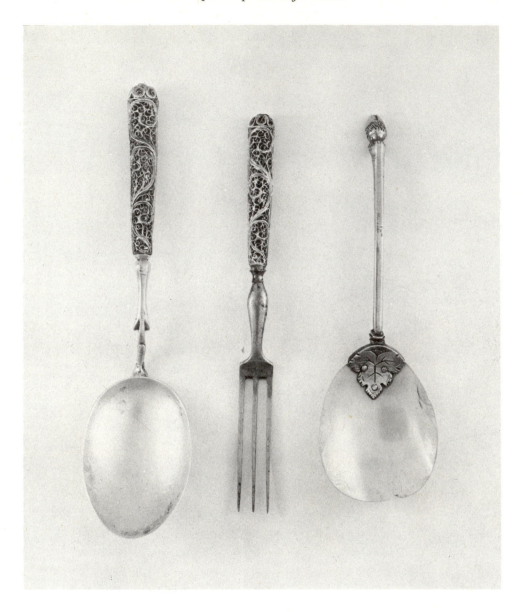

Fig. 80. *Left and centre:* filigree handled spoon and fork, the latter with steel tines. Marked for Augsburg, maker's mark indistinct, c. 1670. There was probably originally a knife to match. A similar set is known with Paris marks for c. 1650. Length of spoon 16 cm., weight 32 grams. *Right:* hoof end with mother-of-pearl bowl. Probably German, the hoof being turned down, mid seventeenth century.

Fig. 81. Three trefids. *Left:* decorated and with an inset coin of Johann Georg, Duke of Saxony, 1628. Town mark a lion, probably Luneberg, maker's mark CL in an oval, engraved 1693, c. 1690. Length 17·6 cm., weight 32 grams. *Centre:* a plainer version engraved with typical East Baltic arms. Warsaw (a mermaid), maker's mark L incuse, c. 1700. Length 17.6 cm., weight 50 grams. *Right:* a horn spoon decorated with pressed ornament featuring steinbock, mounted in silver. Characteristic Salzburg work, c. 1700.

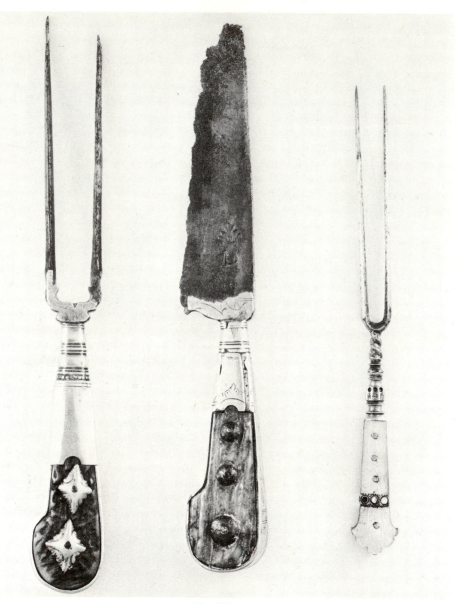

Fig. 82

Fig. 82. *Left and centre:* knife and fork with deerhorn handles mounted in silver, the blade marked D under a crown. Length of fork 18 cm. *Right:* fork with long straight tines and mother-of-pearl handle. All German, mid seventeenth century.

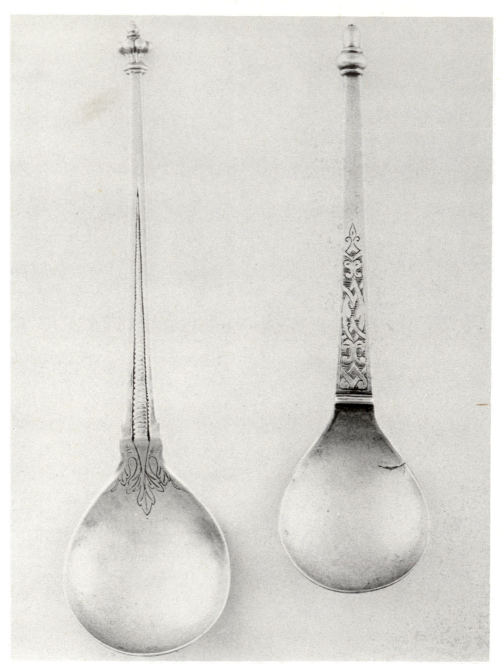

Fig. 83

Fig. 84

Figs. 83–84 (front and back views of same spoons). Two massive Polish soup spoons. *Left:* crown finial, Thorn (T), maker's mark NG. Length 22·4 cm., weight 62 grams. *Right:* acorn finial, punched $_{MW}^{AR}$, an engraved swan between. Length 20 cm., weight 66 grams. Both probably second half of the seventeenth century.

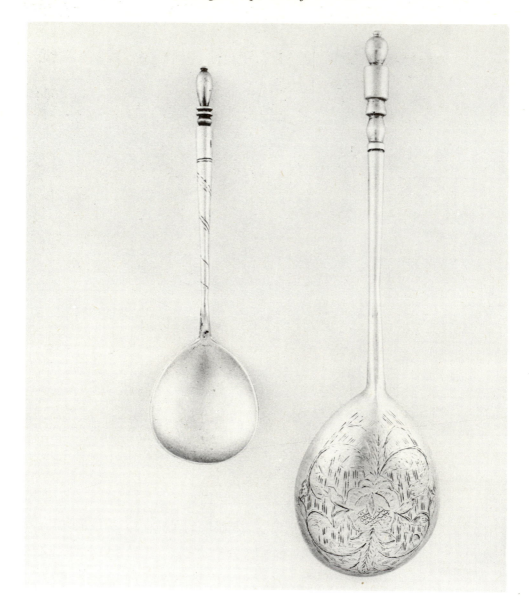

Fig. 85. Two Russian spoons of characteristic shape but unknown age. That on the left has an illegible town mark and a maker's mark B, and is 14 cm in length. The other is unmarked. Many spoons of this pattern were made in the nineteenth century; marked earlier examples are very hard to find.

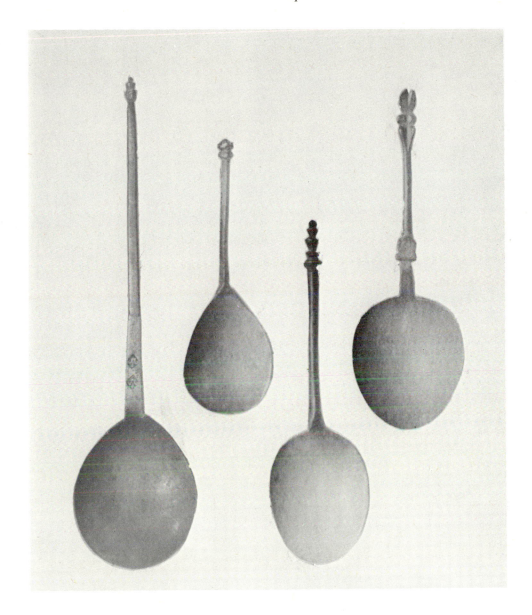

Fig. 86. Four early base metal spoons, brass or bronze, all probably French. The left-hand one is hammered from sheet, with two marks. Length 17 cm. Hague, Gemeente Museum. The remainder are cast. Paris, Musée des Arts Décoratifs.

Fig. 87. Three early French ficulate spoons. *Left:* slip end, with a long tail behind the bowl, mark a crowned letter above a crowned fleur-de-lys, Paris, probably mid fifteenth century, although the form is known from c. 1410. The tip was originally gilt. Length 15·2 cm., weight 28 grams. *Centre:* pine cone finial, marked low down on one facet of the stem with a crowned letter, possibly O, short tail to the stem, c. 1450. Length 16·4 cm, weight 42 grams. *Right:* slip end, with more oval bowl. Marked at the tip for Rouen (a lamb) above an unreadable maker's mark, on another facet a crowned D which may be an assayer's mark; c. 1580. Length 15·2 cm., weight 32 grams.

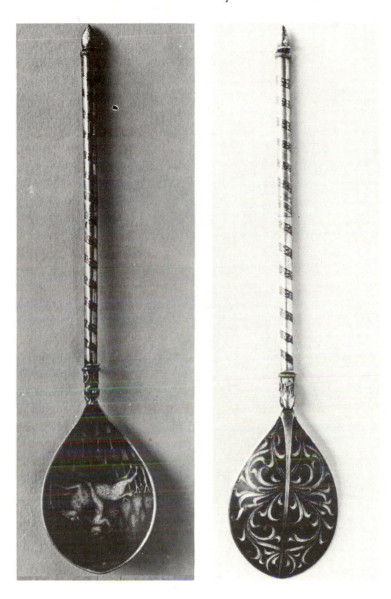

Fig. 88. Front and back views of enamelled silver spoon with animal's head junction, probably Burgundian, fifteenth century. British Museum photograph.

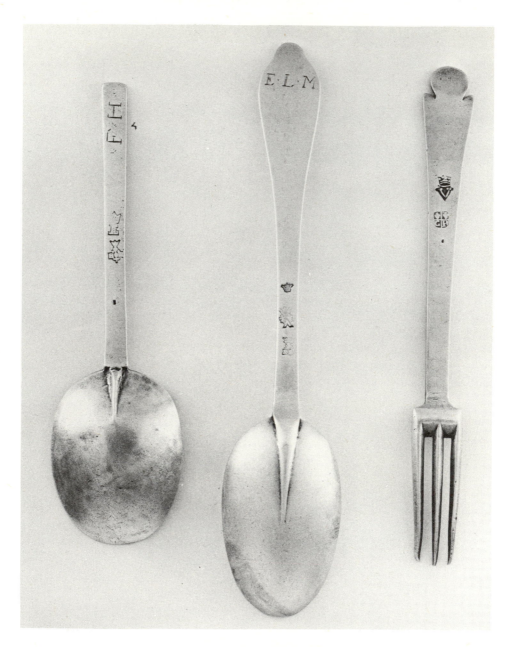

Fig. 89. *Left:* French notched-top Puritan, Paris 1621 (E), maker's mark HR. A form closely related to, and probably followed by, English Puritans. Length 16·1 cm., weight 43 grams. *Centre:* wavy end, Paris c. 1680 (cf. Rosenberg, nos. 6451 and 6452). Maker's mark that of Robert Barbedor, died 1680 (cf. Rosenberg, no. 6638). This spoon shows the lead which Paris had over London at this time. Length 20·8 cm., weight 60 grams. *Right:* fork with trilobate end, Clermont Ferrand, maker's mark CP below two fleur-de-lys for Charles Payen. Length 17·8 cm., weight 49 grams. *Catalogue de l'Orfevrerie du Louvre et de Musée de Cluny,* Paris 1958.

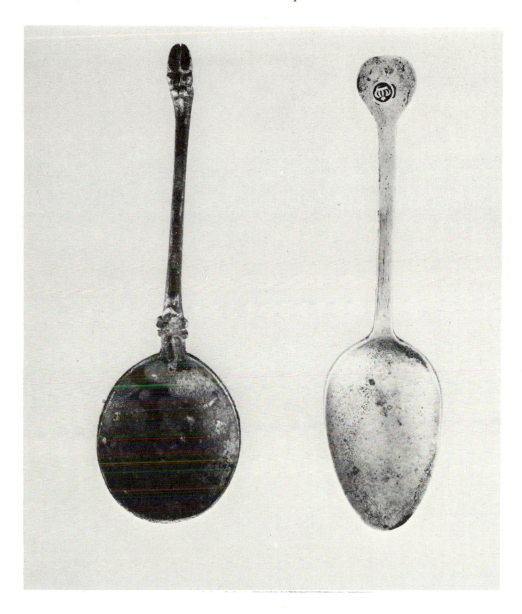

Fig. 90. *Left:* pewter spoon with hoof end, not quite characteristically Dutch or German, possibly French, early to mid seventeenth century. *Right:* brass spoon with disc end punched with a maker's mark—one of many seen. French c. 1700, probably reflecting an earlier version in silver. Length 16·6 cm.

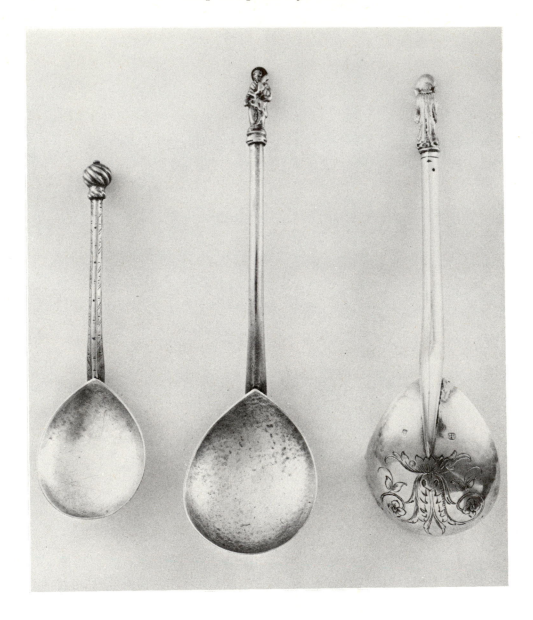

Fig. 91. Three early seventeenth century Swiss spoons with hollow curved stems. *Left:* wrythen knop, maker's mark DW for Daniel Weiss, Berne, born 1582, died 1653. Length 12·2 cm. *Centre:* St Bartholomew, maker's mark O. Length 17 cm., weight 30 grams. *Right:* St Andrew, probably Neuchatel. The apostle finials are from unmutilated patterns of the Dutch 'small headed' series. The shape is highly characteristic of Switzerland.

Fig. 92. *Left:* spoon with maplewood bowl and silver sleeve, probably Swiss, c. 1600. Length 14·6 cm. *Centre:* spoon with hollow twisted stem, Zug, maker's mark AI, c. 1660 (cf. Brunner: *Old Table Silver,* Fig. 222). Length 16·8 cm., weight 24 grams. *Right:* horn spoon with twisted stem and characteristic long inscription; probably eighteenth century.

Fig. 93. A selection of early horn spoons dug up from occupation sites in Friesland. Reproduced to half actual size. Fries Museum, Leeuwarden.

6

The Golden Age of the Netherlands

SPOONS have a special significance for the people of the Netherlands, because of the custom of presenting a child at its christening with a birth-spoon (*gebortelepel*): these gifts were often treasured as family heirlooms, preserving for study a large number of early examples. Unfortunately, only silver spoons were cherished in this way, and as Dutch silver spoons made before the year A.D. 1600 are virtually unknown, the study of earlier forms is extremely difficult.

The custom has had two further effects. The first is the production of spoons which are almost wholly ornamental, and whose design is unrelated to that of those used at the table: such spoons, their stems often formed as boats or windmills, are common in the shops today. The second is the making, to satisfy conservative tastes, of 'replicas' of early spoons, which range from the respectable copy (bearing a modern hallmark) to the deliberate fake, marked with false punches simulating those in use in the seventeenth century. Some of these fakes have found their way into museums, as well as into private collections: they very seldom copy accurately all the features of any one early spoon, but are often sufficiently convincing to make even the expert think twice. Much good work has been done in recent years in exposing these impostors, but very many remain in circulation: their existence makes necessary an attitude of extreme suspicion when confronted with an unusual specimen, and it is likely that some perfectly genuine spoons are condemned simply for lack of corroborative evidence of their origin.

The history of spoons in the Netherlands is divisible into three clearly marked periods. Material attributable to the first of these, from Roman times to the close of the sixteenth century, is extremely scarce and is northern European rather than Dutch —in fact, it is not possible to say with certainty which, if any, of these early spoons were made within the present boundaries of the country. The second period begins with the sudden access of wealth to the United Provinces which followed the revolt against Spain and the success of the East and West India Companies. It occupies roughly the seventeenth century and produced a bewildering profusion of styles adapted from many sources and frequently highly localised: it is of outstanding interest not only for the spoons themselves, but for the evidence of cultural contacts which they supply. This period has received the concentrated attention of the makers of fakes, adding confusion to a situation already sufficiently involved. The third period begins towards the close of the century with the introduction (probably from France) of the form of spoon which was eventually to supersede all others, and to evolve into the kind currently in use—an evolution which was virtually complete by 1730. Spoons of the earlier patterns have been made continuously since, but they are not for everyday use and have little artistic or historical interest.

Throughout the past four centuries spoons of wood, horn and pewter have been made to a simple pattern which certainly antedates the earliest silver. Little relationship is evident between these and the silver forms—in seeking for inspiration the silversmiths of the golden age appear to have looked everywhere but in their own homes. There can be little doubt that the design of pewter follows that of the wood, and that those made of silver were always in a very small minority. Spoons of brass and horn are rare today, but both must have predominated in the early years of the seventeenth century.

The practice of assaying and marking silver did not develop in the Netherlands until the beginning of the second period, and then was irregular and uncoordinated until 1663, when a uniform standard mark and date letter were instituted: unfortunately the date letters of successive cycles resembled one another so closely that considerable uncertainty sometimes remains as to the year in which a marked piece was made. It is also unfortunate—from the collectors' point of view—that no penalties exist to deter those who forge early marks: in this respect British law, which imposes a sentence of up to fourteen years' imprisonment for such forgery, is notably more strict.

While the evidence from hallmarks may be ambiguous, that from contemporary artists, though scanty, is more positive: spoons are portrayed in many pictures by Jan Steen, and in one or two cases a clearly recognisable portrait of a particular type antedates the earliest known specimen.

The great interest of Dutch spoons arises from the fact that they were made by silversmiths untrammelled by traditions either of form or of construction. Faced with a sudden demand they produced more varieties in one century than most countries ever produced at all. Some were difficult to make, some to use—others were weak and failed in service: by the end of the seventeenth century the public must have tired of exotic designs, and the succeeding spoons were sober but practicable variants of the basic pattern in use today.

THE EARLY PERIOD

A detailed study of the spoons of the Netherlands only becomes possible after about 1600; there is very little evidence to show what types were in use before then. The majority were undoubtedly of wood or horn (Fig. 93), of the simple shapes common to the rest of northern Europe, and illustrated in a picture by Peter Aertz (1509–1575) in the Rijksmuseum. Some simple pewter spoons, subsequently referred to as the Jan Steen pattern (Fig. 94) because of their frequent occurrence in his peasant interiors, may be sixteenth century, but the pictures in question date from about 1660. The pattern strongly suggests derivation from a wooden original very like a modern cooking spoon.

A wide variety of flat-stemmed brass spoons of late mediaeval type is found in the Netherlands (e.g. Figs. 43, 44). They are generally known as *geuzenlepels*, after the guerilla bands or *geuzen* which operated against the Spaniards in the sixteenth century, but many appear to be considerably earlier, and at least one has been found in an excavation associated with fourteenth-century pottery. They are probably all of Flemish origin, from near Liege.

In a country which was repeatedly over-run by foreign armies, it is not surprising that an odd mixture should occur, and brass spoons of English, French and Italian aspect are found together in museums and shops. They are of interest for their possible influence on later designs in silver, but it seems unlikely that any were made within the boundaries of the present Netherlands.

No entirely satisfactory example of a silver spoon of Netherlandish origin is known which can definitely be dated before 1600. There are a few debatable ones, but they do not give any coherent picture of development, and the authenticity of some is very doubtful.

THE SEVENTEENTH CENTURY

In the years which followed the revolt against Spain, craftsmen in large numbers migrated from the southern provinces to the north, where they were joined by Huguenot refugees from France. The prosperity which followed, which was accelerated by the growth of the great trading companies, affected the northern seaports first; it is thus not surprising to find that the great majority of early silver spoons come from Friesland and Groningen, Hoorn and Enkhuizen, and Amsterdam. In the prevailing conditions, the craftsmen of each region formed a tightly-knit community having apparently little contact with those of other regions, and this led to the evolution of distinctive local shapes and forms of decoration.

In looking for patterns, the local silversmiths had little to guide them in the way of tradition. They apparently disdained to elaborate the simple wooden and pewter spoons in general use, and instead borrowed freely from Scandinavian, German, Italian and French sources, modifying the designs to produce local variants, but never achieving any unity of style. There is no characteristic Dutch spoon of the period, but instead there are seven or more distinct types, differing in original inspiration as well as in construction, and sometimes narrowly confined to a small region and a short period. It is this which makes some formal system of classification essential.

CLASSIFICATION

Any system of classification for a series of objects as miscellaneous as Dutch spoons must necessarily be open to criticism. Previous attempts have been on the basis of the terminal,[1] of use, or even of authenticity. The first is highly unsatisfactory, as different terminals are found on otherwise identical spoons; the second ignores the fact that the same spoon may have many uses, while the third introduces an element of opinion which is disputable. The classification here put forward is based on the method of construction, and in particular on the relationship of the bowl and stem; this gives five major groups:

1. Bowl and stem in one piece, formed usually by hammering from thick bar, but occasionally by casting; the stem is generally as deep as it is wide; this is the type already designated ficulate.

2. Bowl hammered from sheet, soldered to a hollow stem also made from sheet; because of very close resemblances, spoons of identical shape but with solid stems are placed in this group, together with those having hollow silver stems and wood or rock-crystal bowls.

3. Bowl and sometimes all or part of the stem hammered from sheet, the rest of the stem being flat and tapering towards the tip. This is a very large group, containing many sub-groups, all apparently derived from a single archetypal form—the horn spoon of the Northern belt.

4. Oval bowl, soldered to a cast stem of generally triangular cross section, with a strengthening tail underneath and a distinctive terminal. This group is quite clearly derived from the hoof-ended spoons of Pompeii.

5. Oval bowl, in one piece with a flat stem which widens towards the top. This group includes trefids, wavy ends and the majority of modern shapes.

This classification is inadequate, by itself, to cover the range encountered, and requires considerable elaboration; this has been kept as simple as possible, but it will be appreciated that Dutch spoons are not susceptible to simple organisation. Some idea of the problem involved can be gained from the fact that all the English spoons made between 1400 and 1600, and classified into dozens of types in such monumental works as How's *English and Scottish silver spoons*, would fall into a single sub-group of group 1.

Group 1—subdivisions

Aa. Stem perfectly plain and tapering slightly away from the bowl. Finial most commonly a gryphon sejant (Figs. 95–97).

Ab. Stem plain for the half nearest to the bowl, then ornamented, usually by twisting; the two sections are separated by a small collar (Figs. 98 and 99).

Type Aa very closely resembles the ficulates which were the standard pattern in both England and France from the fifteenth century onwards. The Dutch spoons are quite clearly copied from French, rather than from English, originals, apart possibly from the finials—some of which are very English in appearance. Slip ends of this type from Friesland are virtually identical with French ones.

The early finials, such as diamond points and acorns, do not appear to occur. It is just possible that two diamond-points, with zig-zag assay scrapes and back-of-bowl marks, formerly in the Ellis collection,[2] are Netherlands work, but this is not established.

A single example, with Antwerp marks, in the Frederiks collection[3] has been claimed as being of about 1500, but looks later. It is of particular interest as being apparently the only known silver spoon of the 'Jan Steen' pattern which is very common in pewter, having a diamond section lower stem expanding and becoming rounded towards the tip.

The earliest dateable spoon of type Aa is one from Alkmaar (1624);[4] by 1640 they were being made in Haarlem and Amsterdam, but do not appear from further south.

Some, bearing the marks of Fries makers, are probably earlier, but cannot be dated exactly.

A rare variety, with a plain stem and baluster knop in one piece with it, was in the Ellis collection, where it was catalogued as Norwich;[5] it bears full Dordrecht marks for 1595, 1616 or 1637—probably the last. A very similar stem and knop appear on a cowrie-shell bowled spoon in the Hague.

Everything about these spoons is consistent with the suggestion that the style was introduced to the northern Netherlands by Huguenot refugees towards the beginning of the seventeenth century; the traditional method of making them does not appear to have been very popular among silversmiths, and some Amsterdam examples appear to have been cast rather than forged.

The earliest example of type Ab is one in the Hague,[6] marked probably in 1614, but the majority are much later. All have cast baluster or animal finials. Some have the margin of the bowl notched on either side of the stem, but otherwise the bowls and lower stems are just like those of group Aa, apart from a little engraving.

The subdivision of the stem into two parts appears to be derived from the old tradition of Iona spoons, more than four centuries earlier, but by what route it has not proved possible to discover. The general outline, and the method of construction, show the same French influence as the previous group. Since Ab spoons are confined to the province of South Holland and the islands, some Spanish influence is possible— or it may be that they are based on Flemish spoons which have all disappeared. Spoons of similar appearance from the Rhineland are quite differently constructed, with soldered joints under, or close to, the bowl.

Group 2

The majority of these spoons have makers' marks only, and so cannot be exactly dated; where they carry engraved dates or crests, these almost all belong to the first half of the seventeenth century. Practically all were made in Friesland.

The normal pattern, Ba, has a hollow stem made from thin sheet, circular in cross section in the earliest examples, and octagonal later. The knop is almost always a berry (Fig. 100).

Although the construction of these spoons closely resembles that of contemporary Swiss ones, the shapes are notably different.

The saving in weight obtained by making the stem hollow possibly did not justify the work involved, and a number of these spoons are found with solid stems, but otherwise identical; these are classed as Bb, and appear to be a little later.

The remaining sub-group, Bc, contains the composite spoons with bowls and stems of wood (Fig. 101), horn or rock-crystal and silver sleeves ending in finials—usually apostles. As they are never marked, there is some doubt as to where they were made, and it is quite possible that they are all German rather than Dutch. It seems likely but by no means certain, that types Ba and Bb evolved from such composite spoons; this is the reason why they are included here.

Group 3

The next group, 3, having round bowls and flat tapering stems, contains many sub-groups, some of which are very localised. All belong to the north European family based on spoons made of horn, such as are sometimes found in the terps of Friesland.

Ca. The stem tapers throughout its length, and is in one piece with the bowl (Figs. 102, 103). Particularly characteristic of Hoorn, this type is also known from Enkhuizen, Groningen, Purmerend and Amsterdam. Close relatives are found from Poland and from Køge in Denmark.

Cb. The bowl and lower stem are identical with those of Ca; the upper stem is formed from one or more twisted wires, or may be twisted from the same piece of metal as the rest of the spoon (Figs. 104, 105 and 106). Distinctive varieties are found from Hoorn, Bolsward and Sneek. In all three cases, the lower stem is engraved, usually with a scrolling pattern, and the finial is either a gryphon or lion sejant or an apostle.

No fully marked spoon of Ca or Cb type is known earlier than 1640, but some rather light unmarked ones give the impression of being older than this. There is a clear relationship to the very much earlier Iona and Rouen spoons, as well as to the *geuzenlepels* previously mentioned. In cases where the finial is missing, Dutch spoons of group Cb could readily be confused with contemporary specimens from Bergen, but the latter never have apostle or animal terminals.

Cc. Spoons of this sub-group have a similar outline to those of Cb, but the stem is made as a casting, ornamented on the front and plain on the back, which is attached to the bowl with a long scarfed joint; in a few late spoons the stem is continued under the bowl as a tail, and one example is known with a separate stiffening rib.

There are several stem patterns. One of the commonest features a bird and fruit, with a cherub's head where the narrow upper stem joins the lower. This occurs in an Emden spoon of 1616[7] and another of 1624 (Figs. 107, 108), and from 1630 is found from Leeuwarden in a very slightly retouched version. The same basic pattern was used at Groningen, but the cherub's head was partly cut away and replaced by an architectural moulding (Fig. 109). A slightly different fruit pattern, which gives the impression of being by the same hand, is found on another Groningen spoon of 1625 (Fig. 109); it recurs later, but is rare. Identical in outline, but very different in effect, is a pattern exclusive to Groningen in which the front of the stem is decorated with overlapping scales (Figs. 113, 114); this is seen on a spoon of 1615 in the museum at Groningen, and remained popular until the middle of the century.

The majority of the Cc spoons have apostle finials, but there are a few balusters, cherub head knops and lion sejants.

Cd. This is a small sub-group, containing some not entirely convincing spoons, none of which are fully marked. The stem is of roughly square section, prolonged as a rat tail under the bowl, the lower part sometimes decorated with scales; the finials are apostles or lions. The makers' marks on these spoons are generally assigned to Friesland, but the scale pattern suggests a Groningen origin. The fact that Groningen was the original home of the notorious faker de Haas is an added reason for treating some of these spoons with reserve.

Ce. The outline is as for Cb, but the spoons are very much heavier, the stem patterns are different, and the stem is invariably prolonged under the bowl as a short, thick tail (Figs. 115, 116, 117). All the Netherlands spoons of this class are from Enkhuizen, but some are known with apparently German marks,[8] and the inspiration is certainly German. The Enkhuizen spoons are heavy and coarse, but are of interest for the wide variety of figure finials which they carry, representing a large number of different tradesmen as well as allegorical personages such as Hope; some of these appear on Hoorn spoons of the early eighteenth century.

There is a strong family resemblance between these Enkhuizen spoons and some made in Breslau in the latter part of the previous century.

Group 4

Group 4, while very numerous, is at least coherent; it includes all those spoons having oval bowls soldered to cast stems, and quite clearly derives from the Italian hoof ends, and thence from Roman times. There are four sub-groups:

Da. Hoof ends (Figs. 121 and 122). These closely resemble the Italian prototypes, the chief difference being in the realistic tooling of the hoof and foreleg. The earliest specimen so far recorded is one of 1648 (Groningen), but a picture by W. C. Heda, ascribed to 1637 (in the Louvre), shows one very clearly, and as the type is known with English marks as early as 1607, and Antwerp ones of 1626 (Fig. 120), there is no reason why even older ones should not be found. The form remained popular well after the middle of the century, particularly in the north. Some interesting variations were made in Groningen between 1650 and 1670.

Db. Figure terminals. After about 1660, the hoof began to be replaced by figures—first a grotesque half-figure (Figs. 123, 124), then well-modelled representations of allegorical personages such as Justice, Hope, Charity and Plenty (Figs. 125, 126, 127), with a sprinkling of figures of William II holding his baton, and a few late examples showing William and Mary. All these figures give the impression of having been modelled in the same workshop, possibly in Amsterdam.

Dc. A further crop of terminals includes volute ends, monkeys, and a series of tradesmen; these were particularly popular at Hoorn and Enkhuizen, but are found from most areas (Fig. 123).

In all these three varieties the bowls and lower stems are generally identical. The patterns for the stems were made in two halves, which could be interlocked in the middle to enable any combination to be produced. The join is always represented by a slight bulge, possibly caused by wax reinforcement, and often the V is clearly visible on the back of the finished casting. A large number of these patterns have been preserved in the silversmith's shop in the Fries Museum.

In a few cases the whole stem was cast from a single pattern; this certainly applies to some spoons with hoof terminals on knobbled stems, found chiefly from Groningen, and to a set of eight, with birds' head finials, now in the Rijksmuseum.

In the last sub-group, Dd (Fig. 128), the stem was modified to an open twist; terminals were generally allegorical figures, but in the eighteenth century ships and windmills appear. These spoons were not intended for everyday use, and are often found in mint condition. They are very common, and are indeed still in production as *gebortelepels*; some have Amsterdam and Fries marks as early as the first quarter of the eighteenth century, a number have Fries makers' marks only, a great many have forged marks, copied with varying degrees of skill, and not a few have English import marks of the late Victorian period.

All spoons of group 4 are also found in pewter, differing very little from those in silver.

Group 5

The last major group, 5, differs from all the others in being forged in one piece, with an oval bowl, a flat stem widening towards the tip, and a long tapering rat tail under the bowl. It includes the trefid and wavy-ended types, both of which are found from about 1675 (Figs. 129, 130).

There is no doubt as to their origin: they resemble very closely the corresponding spoons made in Britain and France a few years earlier. It is just possible that the trefid was introduced from Britain and the wavy end simultaneously from France, since they first appear at the same time, whereas in Britain the wavy end is not found much before 1700, but the inspiration was French in both cases. The earlier origin of the trefid is discussed elsewhere.

Spoons of this form are both easier to make and more practicable to use than those of preceding groups, and it is not surprising that they rapidly ousted the latter for most purposes. After about 1700 the older types were made only as *gebortelepels*, and the flat-stemmed variety evolved, through a series of relatively minor modifications to the junction feature and terminal, into the spoons in common use today. It is significant that the Amsterdam firm of W. Helweg, which has been making spoons continuously since 1753, still uses dies for spoon backs dating back to the early years, and most of the patterns produced today can be matched by specimens with eighteenth-century hallmarks.

Although the majority of group 5 spoons were made in one piece, a few exist in which the bowl and stem are cut separately and soldered together; these are probably early attempts at a new style by silversmiths who had not yet mastered the process of forging in one. There are also some spoons with stems and bowls of trefid type, surmounted by cast terminals such as were used on Group 4; William and Mary figure on several specimens. While many are perfectly genuine, the ease with which a trefid spoon can be 'improved' in this way makes it necessary to view them with mild suspicion, and to apply the usual criteria before accepting them as genuine.

With the earliest wavy-ended spoons are found matching forks—the first wholly separate forks made in the Netherlands. A few combined implements, in which the spoon bowl was made to fit with loops over the tines of a fork, generally folding in the middle, are known of basic Group 3 or 4 form, but they are flimsy, and cannot have been in general use.

This brief account is of necessity based on limited information, but is intended to form a framework on which more can be built. Details of the various types will be found accompanying the plates, and these should make it possible to identify all but the most uncommon varieties. Spoon makers were sometimes individualists, and were not bound rigidly to conform to current fashions.

NOTES

1. J. W. Frederiks: De Nederlandsche Zilveren Lepel voor 1800, *Historia*, Utrecht 1944, spoon No. 10.
2. Sotheby and Co.: Catalogue of the Ellis Collection, 30 May 1935.
3. Frederiks, op. cit., spoon No. 2.
4. Frederiks, op. cit., spoon No. 17.
5. Sotheby and Co.: Catalogue of the Ellis Collection, 13 November 1935, No. 42.
6. Gemeentemuseum, The Hague: Zilver van Haagse Edelsmeden.
7. Frederiks, op. cit., probably spoon No. 9.
8. Bodo Glaub: *Die Kunst und das Schöne Heim*, privately printed, Cologne, pages 3 and 6.

Fig. 94. Two early spoons of types used in the Netherlands before 1600. *Left:* with maple-wood bowl and silver sleeve terminating in an apostle (St James) with nimbus intact. Dutch or North German, c. 1600. Length 17·5 cm. *Right:* pewter spoon of 'Jan Steen' pattern, marked in the bowl with a crowned rose, early seventeenth century.

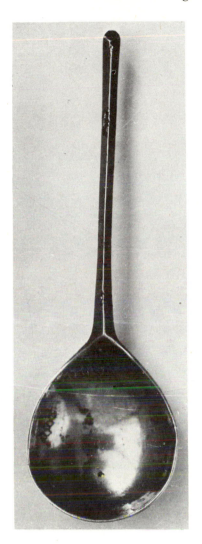

Fig. 95. Front and back views of a Fries slip end spoon of characteristically French pattern, engraved with a Fries marriage double coat of arms (van Oldeberkoop-Osinga). Maker's mark (?) a fox. Engraved 1630. Length 17 cm., weight 41 grams. Fries Museum, Catalogue no. 524.

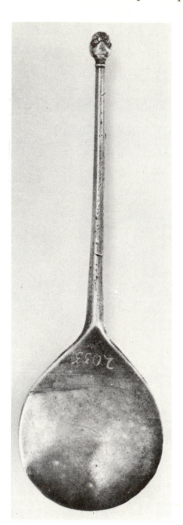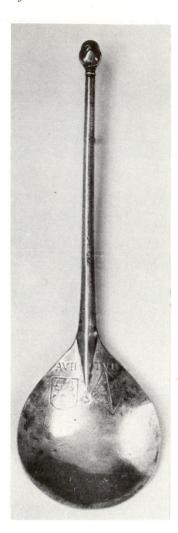

Fig. 96. Front and back view of a Fries one-piece berry finial spoon of type Aa. Maker's mark only, a bird, for Jan Stoffels of Bolsward, early seventeenth century. Engraved with double coat of arms and AVH TVH for the marriage of Antonij van Hettinga and Tieth Douwesdr van Hettinga. Length 16·7 cm., weight 36 grams. Fries Museum, Catalogue no. 521.

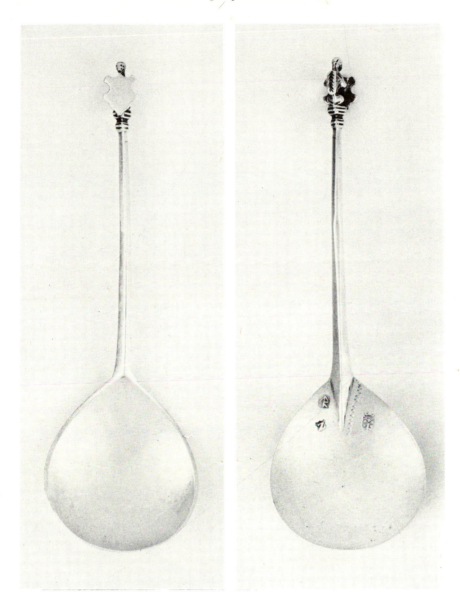

Fig. 97. Front and back view of gryphon sejant, type Aa, Haarlem 1644 (Z), maker's mark a housemark. Length 17·3 cm., weight 36 grams. The earliest recorded specimen is from Alkmaar, 1624 (cf. Frederiks, vol. II, no. 111). The basic form is French, but the gryphon is very characteristic of Holland.

Fig. 98. *Left:* gryphon sejant of type Ab, with later pierced bowl, Delft, mid seventeenth century. Length 16·7 cm, weight 35 grams. *Right:* large baluster finial spoon of type Ab. No marks, possibly South Holland, but conceivably Poland. Length 19·9 cm, weight 57 grams.

Fig. 99. *Left:* bobbin finial spoon, made in one piece. Hoorn 1645 (H).

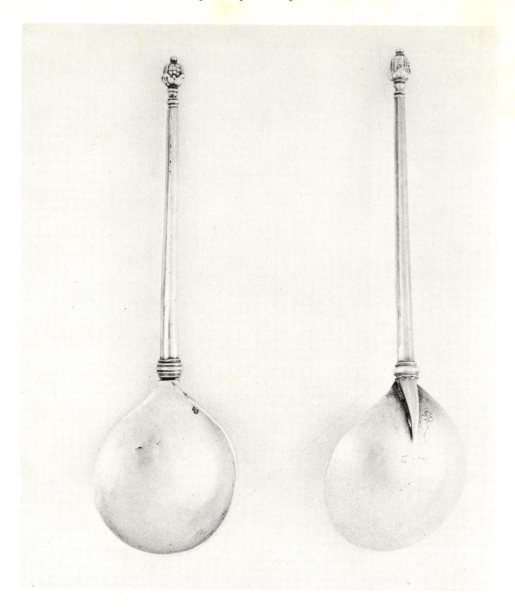

Fig. 100. Two Fries berry knops with hollow stems, type Ba, both Leeuwarden. *Left:* maker's mark a star. Length 17·4 cm., weight 33 grams. *Right:* maker's mark a trefoil for Jan Gerrits. Length 17·7 cm., weight 33 grams. These spoons are characteristic of a small district around Leeuwarden, 1620–1640. Unlike those of similar Swiss spoons (Fig. 91) the stems are straight.

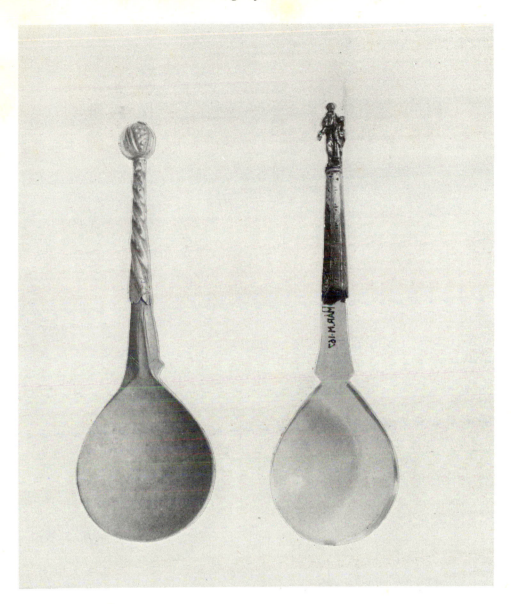

Fig. 101. *Left:* maplewood spoon with silver sleeve and ball knop. German, or possibly Swiss, c. 1600. *Right:* rock-crystal spoon with silver apostle finial (St Peter) of the Dutch series, without nimbus. Probably North Holland or Germany, c. 1620. Cambridge, Fitzwilliam Museum.

Fig. 102

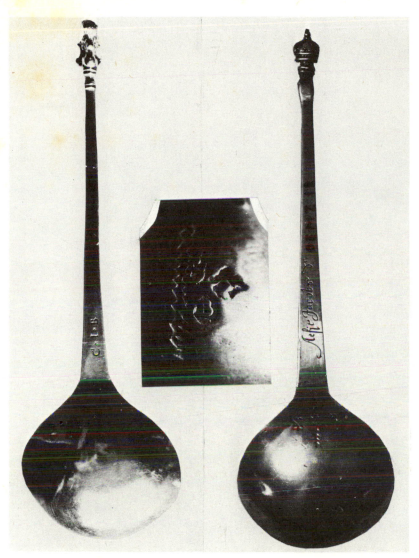

Fig. 103

Figs. 102–103 (front and back views of same spoons). Two spoons from Hoorn. *Left:* lion sejant, with plain tapered stem, marked Hoorn 1645 (M). *Right:* crown finial, the stem engraved with horn motifs, probably 1654 (X) : note how the town mark is struck over the assay scrape. Hague, Gemeentemuseum. *Centre of Fig. 103:* marks from a similar spoon in the Fitzwilliam Museum, Cambridge, showing a different arrangement. Hoorn, apparently 1654.

Fig. 104

Fig. 104. Front and back view of apostle spoon (St James) of characteristic Bolsward pattern, the stem in one piece. Marks for Bolsward 1639 (H). Maker's mark ✗, given in the Fries Museum catalogue—in which this spoon is no. 526—as a housemark. Length 17·5 cm., weight 42 grams. An almost identical spoon, with the figure of St Andrew, in the Rijksmuseum, Amsterdam, has the date letter G, and is attributed to Jacob Jacobs.

Several apostle spoons of similar construction, but unmarked, are known, some of rather crude workmanship. One (St Andrew) in the Rijksmuseum is engraved JOHA ROERDA. ANNA SIVIF, and is very thin, with bowl and stem in one piece; another, in the Fries Museum (no. 5566) bears St Paul and is engraved MR. SUERC. WIL LEMS GAEMA. 1615. Both have the beading along the edges of the stem which is seen on the two definitely Bolsward spoons, suggesting that they may be by the same maker, at a time when he was less skilled.

The resemblance between these Bolsward spoons and those made in Bergen at about the same period is very marked, the difference being mainly in the finials and in the overall length of the stem (see also Figs. 65 and 66). Some specimens in the Gemeente Museum of the Hague, formerly in the Frederiks collection, which are somewhat intermediate between the two, may well be early attempts by Fries silversmiths to copy the Norwegian pattern; they have vase-shaped knops not far removed from the Norwegian ball. It is, however, difficult to establish who copied whom, and it is possible that both Norway and Friesland drew their inspiration from the same external source, probably German.

Fig. 105. *Left:* brass lion sejant spoon of Bolsward pattern, probably Bolsward c. 1640. *Right:* short cast brass or bronze apostle spoon of a pattern found frequently in Holland and Germany: origin unknown, but probably German, seventeenth century. Groningen Museum.

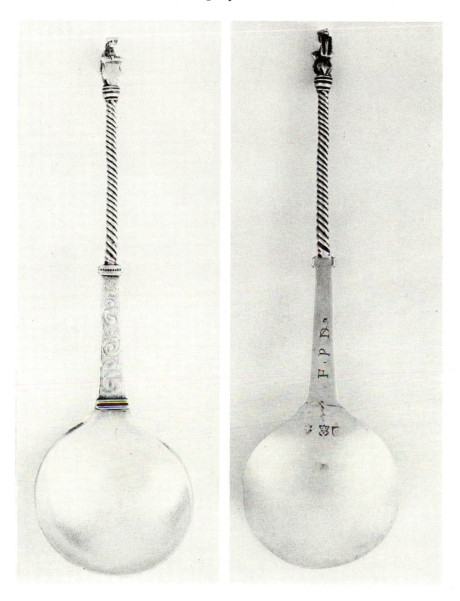

Fig. 106. Front and back view of gryphon sejant of type Cb, Hoorn 1661 (G), maker's mark a trefoil. The bowl and lower stem are in one piece. The upper stem is made from two wires twisted together. Note how the town mark is struck over the zig-zag assay scrape, a feature of Hoorn from c. 1655. Length 19·2 cm., weight 42 grams.

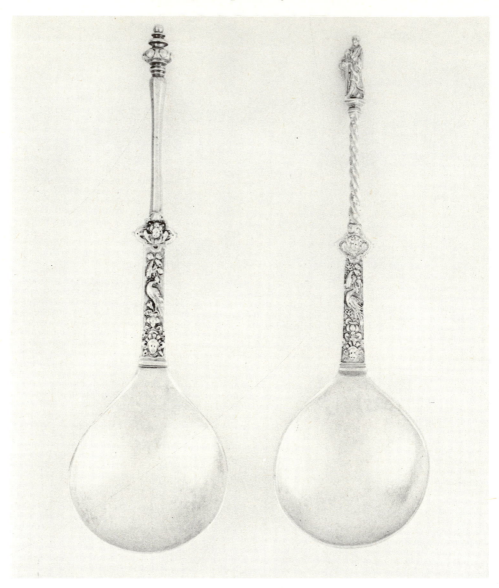

Fig. 107

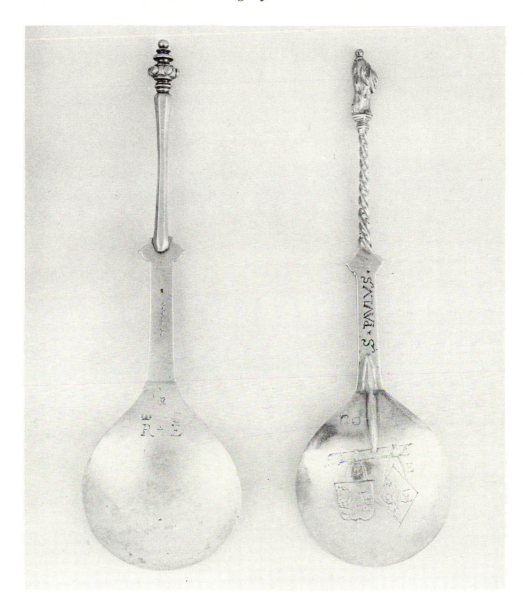

Fig. 108

Figs. 107–108 (front and back views of same spoons). Two spoons of Cc type, with 'bird and fruit' stems. *Left:* baluster knop, Emden 1624 (A), maker's mark a housemark. Length 18·8 cm., weight 48 grams. *Right:* St Paul, Leeuwarden 1632 (A), maker's mark a fleur-de-lys for Jarich Gerrits van der Lely, the first of a notable family of silversmiths. Length 18·6 cm., weight 41 grams.

Fig. 109

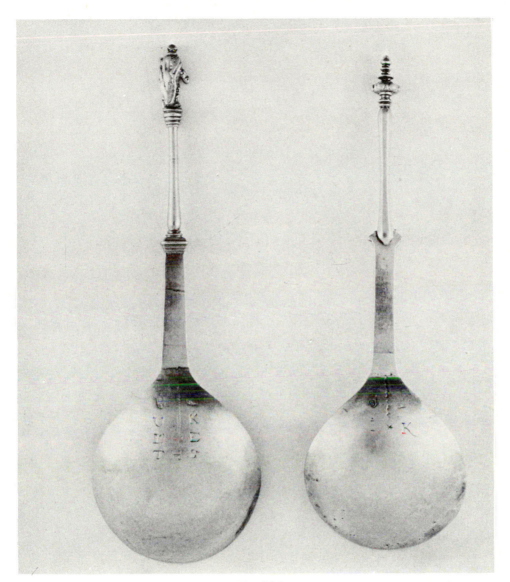

Fig. 110

Figs. 109–110 (front and back views of same spoons). Two Groningen spoons. *Left:* St Peter, 1640 $\left(\frac{2}{1}\right)$, maker's mark NHL conjoined, probably Nicholas Lubbers : the architectural feature in the middle of the stem is a Groningen feature not found from Leeuwarden. Length 18·2 cm., weight 36 grams. *Right:* baluster knop, 1625 (S), maker's mark illegible. Closely resembling the 'bird and fruit' pattern, this variety is much less common. Length 17·4 cm., weight 36 grams.

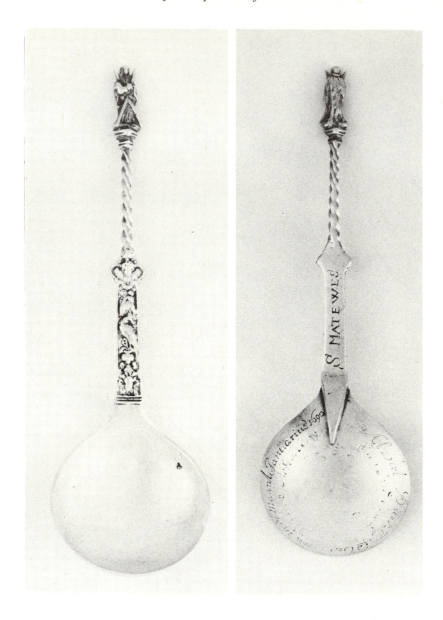

Fig. 111. Front and back view of same spoon. St Andrew on a 'bird and fruit' stem; maker's mark only, a horn, for an unknown Bolsward maker c. 1690. Engraved on the stem S MATEWES, and on the back ALBERT DIRCKS IS GEBOREN IN DE MAANT JANUARIUS 1690 and, in another hand, EN IS IN . . . 2 NOVEMBER 1757. Such double inscriptions are exceedingly rare. No. 566 in the Fries Museum catalogue is an identical spoon, the stem engraved ST WILLEBROD (!). The triangular extension of the stem below the bowl is a late feature, curing an obvious weakness. Length 17·5 cm., weight 36 grams.

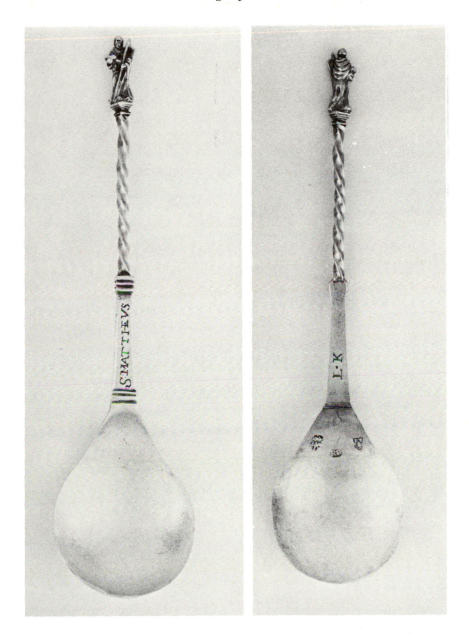

Fig. 112. Front and back views of a somewhat problematical spoon of Cb type, with figure of St Matthew. Town mark double struck, apparently Cologne, maker's mark RR. A third mark resembles that of Norden in East Friesland. The bowl is much worn. The shape of the punches supports the attribution to Cologne. Length 19·5 cm., weight 31 grams.

Fig. 113

Fig. 113. Front and back views of the earliest recorded Groningen spoon, the first of a series characterised by scale pattern stems with mouldings halfway down. The moulding in this case is a separate piece, fitted over the stem and soldered on. The finial is a lion sejant, which is unusual, most similar spoons bearing apostles. Marks for Groningen 1613 (H)—in the first series there is no figure above the date letter. Maker's mark a monogram incorporating M, probably for Muntinck. Groningen Museum.

The origin of the scale pattern is not clear; it has some affinities with the decoration on the stems of the much earlier Iona spoons and, taken with the moulding just above the bowl, might be thought to represent the body of a sea monster of which the moulding is the vestigial head. This would make the architectural feature singularly out of place! It is noticeable that the scales are much larger on this and some other earlier spoons than on those made after 1620.

A rather similar spoon, with lion sejant terminal and scale pattern lower stem, but without the central architectural feature, is illustrated in the catalogue of the Rheinisches Landesmuseum in Bonn (Fig. 13, inventory no. 64,241). It bears the mark of Wesel and is attributed to c. 1600; the catalogue entry refers to a similar spoon with Cologne marks, very possibly by the same maker, in the Museum für Kunst und Gewerbe in Hamburg.

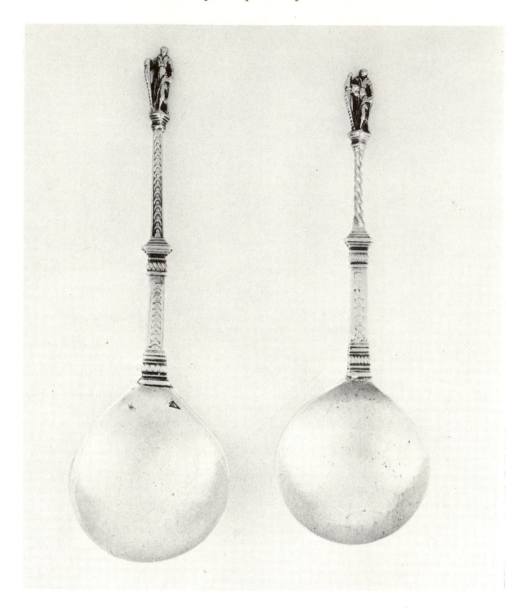

Fig. 114. Two very typical Groningen spoons, both with the figure of St Simon Zelotes and scale pattern stems. *Left:* 1629 (X), maker's mark illegible. Length 18 cm., weight 32 grams. *Right:* maker's mark only, struck twice, MSL conjoined, possibly for a member of the Muntinck family, c. 1625. Length 16·7 cm., weight 31 grams.

Fig. 115. Front and back views of a typical Enkhuizen spoon with finial representing a brushmaker, the lower stem from a much-used pattern, the rat tail short and thick. Marks Enkhuizen, probably 1662 (B), maker's mark a lamb. The Hague, Gemeentemuseum.

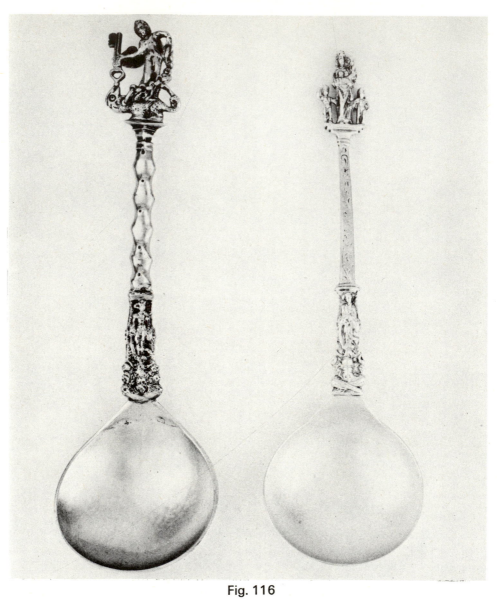

Fig. 116

Fig. 117

Figs. 116–117 (front and back views of same spoons). Two spoons of Enkhuizen type Ce. *Left:* with St Michael and the dragon, Enkhuizen c. 1665 (date letter not clear), maker's mark a tulip. Length 19·8 cm., weight 79 grams. *Right:* maker's mark only, VB or WB, Enkhuizen or Hoorn, probably early eighteenth century. Length 19 cm., weight 56 grams. The long tail behind the bowl is a feature of this pattern, which in the Netherlands is confined to a small region dominated by the East India Company, although specimens are known apparently from Cologne.

Fig. 118

Figs. 118–119 (front and back views of same set). A set of silver sleeves with apostle finials, from spoons of wood, horn or rock crystal, showing the apostles in unmutilated form. Probably North German; if Dutch, before 1620. *Left to right:* Saints Bartholomew, Thomas, Matthew, James, Andrew, Philip (the last almost unknown from Holland, where it was not a popular name in the seventeenth century). The Dutch apostle finials of the group C spoons deserve special attention. Apostles were used as spoon finials in England as early as 1490, but they invariably have the proportions of dolls rather than of adult figures. The Dutch ones are much more realistically proportioned and are finely detailed. They are undoubtedly from the same original patterns as some found on German and Swiss spoons, with the significant difference that the nimbi have been filed away from those used in the Netherlands. This set have nimbi, as have a number of others which are still attached to their spoons, but several rock-crystal and wooden spoons are known without them. When present, the nimbi are set well to the back of the heads, as in the earliest English series; the shift from this position to that of a flat hat which occurs in statues was almost certainly caused by sad experience with birds and, to judge by the well-dated English spoons, was complete by 1550 at the latest, so it would appear that the patterns for the Dutch series were either copied from church statues made before that date, or were made considerably before the first dated spoon on which they appear. The removal of the nimbi may with

Fig. 119

some confidence be put down to the conversion of the northern provinces to Calvinism; it is significant that no complete figure is known on a spoon made after the Synod of Dort in 1617. It seems likely that the original patterns were carved in Germany, and that the Dutch ones were cast from spoons which came into the possession of the local silversmiths. This is very easy to do, and once a casting has been made in brass or even type metal, it can be used for reproduction almost indefinitely. It is even quite a simple matter to build up worn portions with solder, but there is not much indication of this having been done, and certain parts, particularly the heads, show a progressive attenuation. The stem patterns were obviously obtained in the same way. The spoons from Emden have very crisp modelling of the bird-and-fruit pattern, and this may be where it originated. The patterns used at Leeuwarden by Jarich Gerrits van der Lely show slight retouching at one point, and those used at Groningen are more drastically altered at a different place. The ease with which castings can be taken from genuine spoons has led to the production of a large number of fakes. Fortunately, the majority of these are fairly easy to recognise. Perhaps the most important feature to look for is the scarfed joint, which invariably shows some leaching away of the solder line in a genuine spoon. The bowls of early spoons are also much thinner in the middle than at the edges, and always show signs of honest use. Reproduction of these features, while possible, would probably not be economic. Photograph by courtesy of the Rijksmuseum, Amsterdam. Illustrated natural size.

Fig. 120

Fig. 120. Front and back views of lozenge-end spoon of Italian form, but smaller than normal Italian specimens. Marked for Antwerp 1626.

Fig. 121

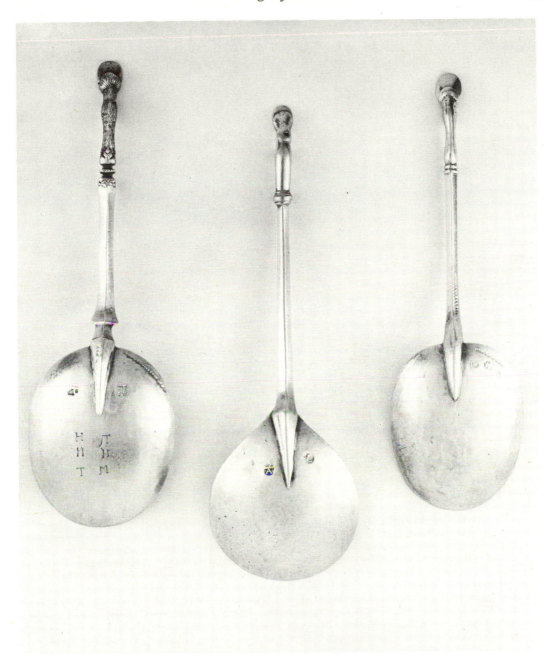

Fig. 122

Figs. 121–122 (front and back views of same spoons). Three hoof ends, type Da. *Left:* Rotterdam 1653 (P), maker's mark a sword, the hoof and foreleg finely tooled. Length 16·8 cm., weight 41 grams. *Centre:* Groningen 1656 $\left(\frac{3}{A}\right)$, maker's mark EL for Egbert Loesinck, a prolific spoonmaker who experimented with many forms. This one is unusual in having the bowl and lower stem of Aa shape, although made in two pieces. Length 17 cm., weight 40 grams. *Right:* probably Kollum, town mark a star, maker's mark a monogram, date letter G, probably 1658. Length 15·8 cm., weight 32 grams. (See also Fig. 17.)

Fig. 123

Fig. 124

Figs. 123–124 (front and back views of same spoons). *Left:* term-figure end, type Db, Amsterdam 1664 (B), maker's mark IP (possibly Jacob Pagendam). Length 17·1 cm., weight 52 grams. *Right:* volute end, type Dc, marks obliterated by repair, c. 1680. Length 15·8 cm., weight 34 grams. Both spoons are clearly derived from Italian originals.

Fig. 125

Fig. 126

Figs. 125–126 (front and back views of same spoons). Two early figure terminals. *Left:* William Stadthouder, maker's mark only, a bell. This spoon retains the early bowl shape. Length 16·7 cm., weight 50 grams. *Right:* Justice (the sword broken, as is usual), Amsterdam 1693, maker's mark not clear. Length 17 cm., weight 42 grams. This form of spoon has been made in Holland continuously since c. 1680.

Fig. 127

Fig. 127. Three figure terminal spoons. *Left:* Charity, on an Amsterdam spoon, 1678 (Q), maker's mark Johannes Pagendam. Length 17·5 cm., weight 41 grams. *Centre:* Plenty, on a Haarlem spoon of c. 1660 (marks rubbed but apparently no lion rampant). Length 17·4 cm., weight 42 grams. *Right:* a fisherman, maker's mark only, Ƶ for Willem Ankes Zestra, Harlingen, born 1661, still working 1729. Length 17·2 cm., weight 46 grams.

Fig. 128

Fig. 128. Three twisted stem spoons. *Left:* Justice, Amsterdam 1754 (U), from the same pattern as the 1693 figure, but showing perceptible shrinkage due to repeated copying; maker's mark FRP. Length 18 cm., weight 66 grams. *Centre:* Mother love, Friesland, maker's mark only: an unidentified device; engraved with a ship and 1699 DEN 22 OCTOBER IS RINTIE JEDDES DOCHTER GEBOREN, AJ in the same hand and MI later. Length 18·2 cm., weight 52 grams. *Right:* Mother love (another version), Amsterdam 1726 (Q), maker's mark a beaked head. Like so many of those made solely as christening spoons, this one is in mint condition. Length 18·8 cm., weight 61 grams.

Fig. 129. *Left:* rat tail spoon, Utrecht, probably 1713 (A), maker's mark DV; the town mark was struck twice on high standard work. Length 19·9 cm., weight 48 grams. *Centre:* fork, double drop pattern, Amsterdam 1735 (A), maker's mark in script for Hendrik Kammerling de Jonge. *Right:* spoon, Louvain c. 1714. Length 19·8 cm., weight 69 grams. Comparison with English cutlery of the same period shows the uniformity which followed the proliferation of styles of the seventeenth century.

Fig. 130. *Left:* trefid, Leyden 1688 or 1712 (B), maker's mark a wheel. *Right:* wavy end with applied ornament, Amsterdam 1737 (C), maker's mark a beaked head. This spoon illustrates the conservatism of Dutch makers—wavy ends were obsolete in Britain by 1712. Length 20 cm., weight 52 grams.

7

Appendices

APPENDIX A

The making of a diamond-point spoon (Figs. Frontispiece, 9 and 131)

THE writer has made many spoons of early form, using different shapes of cast blank and working with the metal hot and cold. In many cases it has been very difficult to distinguish the results from originals except by the absence of a convincing patina. This does not guarantee that the sequence of operations used was identical with that employed by fifteenth-century makers, but it does at least work.

The starting point is a blank about $2\frac{1}{4}''$ (57 mm) long, either round or square in cross section. A round blank with a diameter of $\frac{3}{8}''$ (10 mm) is adequate for a small spoon, but leaves nothing in hand for mistakes; a square section bar is easier to work with. These bars are cast into open holes made by pushing a suitable steel rod into well-packed moulding sand, but stone and charcoal moulds have also proved successful. A metal mould tends to chill the silver too much, so that it develops surface flaws which later turn into cracks.

The bar is held in short tongs, so that it can be worked hot, and drawn for about half its length over a convex anvil matching the radius of the collet hammer used; it is possible to work on the flat of the anvil, but not so easy if a large integral finial is to be produced. In the drawing down, hammering is started close to the end and continued to the middle before turning the blank through ninety degrees and starting again.

It is at this stage that the first problem occurs. If the blank is not turned through exactly ninety degrees before starting the next run, it rapidly develops a lozenge section which is extremely hard to correct, and which very rapidly gets worse. This suggests that the reason why English spoons commonly have hexagonal rather than square stems is the extreme difficulty of drawing down a square; if a lozenge section develops, the obvious way to correct it is to start a third run of hammering onto the acute angles, and once this is done it is quite easy to maintain any desired proportions to the hexagon formed by varying the amount of hammering in the three directions.

French and Dutch silversmiths seem to have overcome this problem successfully—as it can indeed be overcome by very careful aiming of the blows in the early stages; however, it is noticeable that the stems of their spoons, while nominally square, are seldom accurately so, and generally show a slight front and back facet which suggests the need for some correction. Italian brass and bronze spoons often have stems which are distinctly rhomboidal, deeper than they are wide.

At a fairly early stage the shaping of the knop is taken in hand; this is done basically by resting the stem at 45° over the rounded edge of the anvil and hammering down on each facet in turn. If the shaping is left too late, the usual result is to crack the finial away altogether.

Work on the bowl is not begun until the stem is finished. The first stage is to hold the blank on the flat anvil with the front and back facets accurately horizontal and mark the junction of bowl and stem by a single blow from a collet hammer. The flattened portion so produced is continued along towards the tip, leaving the future bowl about half an inch wide and rather less than half as thick. This has to be done very carefully, otherwise the stem facets will not be symmetrically disposed.

Widening of the bowl now proceeds, using the same collet hammer, until it is as thick all over as it is ultimately intended to be at the edges. At this stage a ball-pene hammer is brought into play, and the bowl is thinned in the middle, leaving the edges untouched and always hammering from what is to be the inside. This not only modifies the bowl outline to the familiar fig shape, but also curves it down in the middle into a rudimentary spoon.

Once the bowl is brought to thickness, it can be deepened as necessary by hammering over a block of wood, set with the end grain vertical. The shoulders are sharpened up by hammering into the bowl while the spoon is resting with its axis at about 30° to the edge of the anvil, working on the two sides alternately.

It is possible to finish the bowl over a mushroom-shaped steel stake with either a flat hammer or a mallet, but examination of early spoons leaves some doubt as to whether this was generally done. It seems more likely, from such hammer marks as remain, that all the finishing was done from the inside.

It is possible, by using a blank of the right size and working carefully, to finish a spoon to shape with hardly any trimming of the edges of the bowl; these were finally levelled off with a file, and the whole spoon was burnished by rubbing a piece of hard and polished material—probably steel, but some kinds of hard stone can be used instead—over the surface. This produces a slightly rippled effect which is visible sometimes on the stems of early spoons, in places where they have not been much worn.

It is very difficult to tell how much final polishing was done, as its effects have always been destroyed by wear and solution. Lacking modern methods of treatment of wastes, early makers would be most unwilling to remove more metal at this stage than was absolutely necessary, and abrasive polishing was probably avoided as far as possible.

The gilding of the finial is done by smearing it over with an amalgam of gold and mercury, made to the consistency of butter. This is well rubbed into the surface with a very stiff brush (a small stick cut off square and hammered on the end is very suitable), and after removal of surplus amalgam the mercury is driven off by heating to just below redness. The intensely poisonous fumes given off must have constituted a major hazard to the health of the apprentices who did this part of the work, until a rudimentary type of fume cupboard was devised to contain them. The gold is left in a matt condition, alloyed with the underlying silver to a depth which depends on the time taken over the process; it is burnished in the same way as the rest of the spoon, when it takes on its normal colour.

Gilding done in this way, unlike that done by electro-deposition, wears gradually paler instead of suddenly through, and shows rough patches where excess amalgam remained in corners after wiping off, and was subsequently not reached by the burnish. Both characteristics are often seen in the gilding of apostle and seal finials, and enable mercurial gilding to be recognised. However, this must not be taken as evidence of authenticity by itself, as there is nothing to stop anybody from doing mercurial gilding today—except the much greater expenditure of gold and trouble involved.

It is much easier to put a convincing-looking mark on a spoon than to make the spoon itself. A punch cut in quite soft material—mild steel, or even brass—will make a large number of satisfactory impressions, and some devices very similar to those used in early times can be cut with a minimum of skill. The majority of very early spoons are unmarked, and those which bear marks of any kind generally fetch greatly enhanced prices at auction.

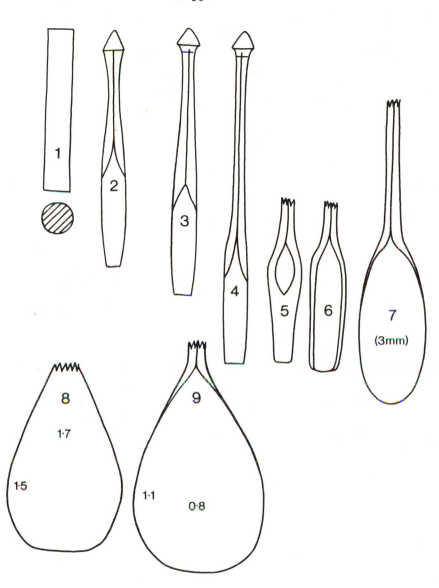

Fig. 131. Stages in making a diamond-point spoon from round bar. The thicknesses are given in millimetres. The finished spoon is shown in Fig. 9.

Brass foundry work in mediaeval Italy

The extract which follows is taken from Book I of Vannuccio Biringuccio's *De la Pirotechnia*, written about 1430. See note 4 of the section of this book, 'Of Spoons in General'. It is an account of work in a brass foundry in Milan. The book deals in considerable detail with all manner of useful arts involving fire, and is a delightful mixture of clear and well-tried practical instructions and old wives' tales—the latter in many cases quite evidently regarded by the author with some scepticism. The details in this extract are of great interest, since they represent meticulous observation by an expert of a process which was probably in general use from classical Greek times until the sixteenth century, and which was probably responsible for many of the Italian spoons illustrated in this book.

'Amongst other things I saw a kind of workman whose method was entirely new to me. There were eight masters near others in a room who did nothing but mould in lute* and form an infinite number of moulds of all those little objects of everyday use which can be made from brass by casting. They made these in such a fine way that I cannot fail to tell you about it. These masters took the number of patterns of all the things that they had decided to mould, that is, harness buckles, cups, belt buckles, all kinds of chain links, bells, thimbles, window fastenings, and other similar things. On one day they made all of one kind and the next day all of another, and thus they proceeded, changing the pattern every day; and having finished one that they had to mould, they began again at the beginning with another, continuing always with this easy method and process of moulding to accomplish much work.

They took a large quantity of lute mixed with cloth clippings or cane seed and, when they had beaten the quantity they wished to use until it was somewhat hard, they spread it out about half a *dito*† thick or less on a little board which was a *palmo*† in length and somewhat wider than the patterns. After having spread it out well, they dusted it with fine charcoal, and in it they moulded their patterns all attached to the gate, with vents, openings, and all parts which are needed to make a complete mould. Some of these patterns were of tin and some of brass, accurately made, filed, and well finished, for if once the mould was well made the objects had to come out the same way. Each of these masters had also near him a small square oven of sheet iron. This was lined with bricks or covered with clay and had a little grate underneath and an open mouth the length of the oven. When a little charcoal and fire was put inside on top of the grate it heated the oven and kept it hot. Then they put the fresh half mould that they had just made to dry above the opening where there was a little grid. While it was drying they made another, and in the same manner when it was made they put it near to the first one, and so they continued up to six or eight pieces. Then they again took up the first one (which had had sufficient heat and time to become dry or nearly so) and on top of this they made the other companion, and on top of this companion they moulded other patterns on the outside. They did the same with all the others and then beginning again from the first one they continued on to all the others in succession, so that when the moulds were finished and were drying one on top of the other they were altogether half a *braccio* or more in height and about half a *palmo* wide, or as wide as a board or the particular pattern, for no useless space should be left around them. After these were finished and well dried in an oven like those where bread is baked, they opened them again, layer by layer, and took out the patterns. These gave twenty or more pieces to each mould, resulting in a great number, for some patterns contained as many as fifty or sixty pieces. Finally, after having closed the moulds again and sealed them up, and after having repaired or retouched the gates or any other points where it was necessary, and having given them a wash of fine ashes and water, they put the moulds together again and returned them exactly to their original position, then they bound them very well with iron wires and sealed them with the same lute. Then they took sixteen or twenty of these moulds and, standing them up on the ground all together, they made a circle of rocks around them and covering all the moulds with charcoal they baked them again. After having baked and arranged them well and having made in each part of the mould a gate which would convey the metal to the gates of all the other moulds, they took them to the furnace where the copper was coloured. When they took one or two of those crucibles from the furnace they filled the mass of the moulds with that well-melted, yellow-coloured copper. They did this singly, or in pairs, or several at a time, according to the number of moulds, filling all the moulds made by the masters whom I have described above. They did this day and night as occasioned by the coloured well-disposed material, or depending on the number of moulds ready.

Pondering on this I thought to myself that this shop alone was sufficient to furnish not only Milan but also the whole of Italy, and surely it seemed to me a splendid and fine undertaking for a single merchant. I thought that he should take great pains to keep alive all the fine undertakings that I saw in that place and continue them and surely it pleased me to see so many things being moulded continuously, and continuously being cast. I believe that no similar work is done in Flanders or in other places in Germany where they make candlesticks, cups, and many other things as they do. Many in those parts are not as advanced as we are.

I have decided to tell you in its proper place among the semiminerals about the earth that colours copper into brass by its peculiar properties.'

* lute = a fine clay

† half a dito = about $1\frac{1}{4}$ inches (3·0 cm)

  a palmo = about 8″–10″ (20–25)

  These dimentions would depend on the articles being cast. Some moulds would be much thinner.

8

Select Bibliography

THERE are very many publications on silver which touch briefly on spoons, but give little detailed information; these have been omitted from this list, which contains only those works which the author has found of real value, either for the information about spoons specifically, or for the marks by which early silver may be identified. Publications dealing almost exclusively with such marks are identified with an M, and those small enough to be carried in the pocket by MP. The bibliography is arranged by countries, following the order used in the text.

GREEK AND ROMAN

Curle, A. O. *The Treasure of Traprain*. Glasgow 1923.
Strong, D. E. *Greek and Roman Gold and Silver Plate*. London 1966.

GENERAL

Brunner, H. *Old Table Silver*. London 1967.
Rosenberg, Marc. *Die Goldschmiede Merkzeichen*, 4 vols., 3rd ed. Frankfurt am Main 1922. The largest and most often quoted book of European marks, identified as R/3. M
Tardy. *Les Poinçons de Garantie Internationaux pour l'Argent*, 8th ed. Paris 1968. Contains extracts from Rosenberg and others. MP
Wyler, Semour B. *The Book of Old Silver: English, American, Foreign*. New York 1949. M

BRITAIN

Banister, Judith. *English Silver Hallmarks*. London 1970. MP
Bradbury, Frederick. *British and Irish Silver Assay Office Marks*. Offered by many shops under their own names. MP
Clayton, Michael. *Collectors' Dictionary of the Silver and Gold of Great Britain and North America*. London 1971.
Cripps, W. J. *Old English Plate*. London 1899, reprinted 1967.
Delieb, Eric. *Investing in Silver*. London 1967.
Finlay, Ian. *Scottish Gold and Silver Work*. London 1956.
Gask, Norman. *Old Silver Spoons of England*. London 1926, reprinted 1973.

Hilton Price, F. G. *Old Base Metal Spoons*. London 1908.

How, G. E. P. and J. P. *English and Scottish Silver Spoons*, 3 vols. London, privately printed, 1952–57.

Jackson, Sir Charles. *Illustrated History of English Plate*. London 1911.

Jackson, Sir Charles. *English Goldsmiths and their Marks*. London 1905, 2nd ed. 1921; 2nd ed. reprinted New York 1964. The bible of collectors and salerooms.   M

Oman, C. C. *English Domestic Silver*. London 1934, 2nd ed. 1947.

Pearl, C. A. *The Connoisseur*, April and July 1970.

Smith, Eric J. G. 'The Early English Silver Spoon', *Antique Collector's Guide*, March 1973.

Snoden, Michael. *English Silver Spoons*. London 1974.

Taylor, G. *Silver*. Harmondsworth 1956.

SCANDINAVIA

Andern, Hellner et al. *Svenskt Silversmide*. Stockholm 1963.   M

Boesen, G. B. and Bøje, C. A. *Old Danish Silver*, trans. R. Kay. Copenhagen 1949.

Bøje, C. A. *Dansk Sølvmaercker*. Copenhagen 1954.   M

Krohn-Hansen, T. *Bergens Gullsmedkunst*. Bergen 1957. Good illustrations and marks.

Krohn-Hansen, T. *Trondheims Gullsmedkunst*. Oslo and Bergen 1963.

Schoubye, S. *Das Goldschmiedehandwerk in Schleswig-Holstein*, 2nd ed. Heide in Holstein 1967.

Upmark. *Gold och Silversmede i Sverige*. Stockholm 1943.   M

FRANCE

Carre, Louis. *Les Poinçons de l'Orfèvrerie Française*. Paris 1928.   M

Cripps, W. J. *Old French Plate*. London 1880.   M

Davis, Frank. *French Silver*. London 1970.

Dennis, Faith. *Three Centuries of French Silver*. New York 1960.

Helft, Jacques. *Les Poinçons des Provinces Françaises*. Paris 1968.   M

Nocq, H. *Le Poinçon de Paris*, 5 vols. Paris 1926–31.   M

GERMANY

Stierling, H. *Der Silberschmuck der Nordseeküste*, 2 vols. 1935–55.

NETHERLANDS

Frederiks, J. W. *Zilverlepel voor 1800*. Historia, Utrecht 1944.

Frederiks, J. W. *Dutch Silver*, 4 vols. The Hague 1952–61.

Fries Museum. *Fries Zilver*. Leeuwarden 1968.

Gans, M. H. and Klinkhamer, ThM, Duyvene de Wit. *Dutch Silver*. London 1961.

Klein, Drs. E. M. C. H. F. *Oude Zilveren Lepels*. Lochem 1967.

Jansen, Beatrice. *Zilver van Haagse Edelsmeden*. 1957. Catalogue of the Haagsgemeentemuseum.

Voet, Elias jr. *Merken van Amsterdamsche Goud- en zilversmeden*. The Hague 1912. M

Voet, Elias jr. *Merken van Friesche Goud- en zilversmeden*. The Hague 1932.   M

Voet, Elias jr. *Namen van Haarlemsche Goud- en zilversmeden*. Haarlem 1903.   M

Voet, Elias jr. *Merken van Haagsche Goud- en zilversmeden*. The Hague 1941.   M

Voet, Elias jr. *Nederlandsche Goud- en zilversmeden*. The Hague 1951.   MP

Index